Immigration Debates in America

CALVIN SHORTS

A series published by the Calvin Press
Titles in the Calvin Shorts Series:

Immigration Debates in America

William Katerberg

CALVIN SHORTS

Calvin PRESS

Grand Rapids, MI • calvin.edu/press

Published 2020 by The Calvin Press
3201 Burton St. SE
Grand Rapids, MI 49546

Unless otherwise noted, Scripture quotations are from the Holy Bible, New International Version®. NIV®. Copyright © 1973, 1978, 1984, 2011 by Biblica, Inc.™ Used by permission of Zondervan. All rights reserved worldwide. www.zondervan.com. The "NIV" and "New International Version" are trademarks registered in the United States Patent and Trademark Office by Biblica, Inc.™

Publisher's Cataloging-in-Publication Data

Names: Katerberg, William H. (William Henry), 1966-, author.
Title: Immigration debates in America / William Katerberg.
Series: Calvin Shorts
Description: Includes bibliographical references. | Grand Rapids, MI: The
    Calvin Press, 2020.
Identifiers: LCCN: 2020934165 | ISBN: 978-1-937555-47-4 (pbk.) |
    978-1-937555-48-1 (ebook)
Subjects: LCSH United States--Emigration and immigration. |
    Immigrants--United States. | Illegal aliens--United States. | Emigration
    and immigration law--United States. | Immigrants--United States--
    History. | United States--Emigration and immigration--History. |
    Minorities--United States--History. | BISAC HISTORY / Social History
    | HISTORY / United States / General | SOCIAL SCIENCE / Emigration
    & Immigration | SOCIAL SCIENCE / Race & Ethnic Relations |
    POLITICAL SCIENCE / Public Policy / Immigration
Classification: LCC E184.A1 .K295 2020 | DDC 305.8/00973--dc23

Cover design: Robert Alderink
Interior design and typeset: Katherine Lloyd, The DESK

Contents

Series Editor's Foreword

Midway along the journey of our life
I woke to find myself in some dark woods,
For I had wandered off from the straight path.

So begins *The Divine Comedy*, a classic meditation on the Christian life, written by Dante Alighieri in the fourteenth century.

Dante's three images—a journey, a dark forest, and a perplexed pilgrim—still feel familiar today, don't they?

We can readily imagine our own lives as a series of journeys: not just the big journey from birth to death, but also all the little trips from home to school, from school to job, from place to place, from old friends to new. In fact, we often feel we are simultaneously on multiple journeys that tug us in diverse and sometimes opposing directions. We recognize those dark woods from fairy tales and nightmares and the all-too-real conundrums that crowd our everyday lives. No wonder we frequently feel perplexed. We wake up shaking our heads, unsure if we know how to live wisely today or tomorrow or next week.

This series has in mind just such perplexed pilgrims. Each book invites you, the reader, to walk alongside experienced guides who will help you understand the contours of the road as well as the surrounding landscape. They will cut back the underbrush, untangle myths and misconceptions, and suggest ways to move forward.

And they will do it in books intended to be read in an evening or during a flight. Calvin Shorts are designed not just for perplexed pilgrims but also for busy ones. We live in a complex and changing world. We need nimble ways to acquire knowledge, skills, and wisdom. These books are one way to meet those needs.

John Calvin, after whom this series is named, recognized our pilgrim condition. "We are always on the road," he said, and although this road, this life, is full of perplexities, it is also "a gift of divine kindness which is not to be refused." Calvin Shorts takes as its starting point this claim that we are called to live well in a world that is both gift and challenge.

In *The Divine Comedy*, Dante's guide is Virgil, a wise but not omniscient mentor. So, too, the authors in the Calvin Shorts series don't pretend to know it all. They, like you and me, are pilgrims. And they invite us to walk with them as together we seek to live more faithfully in this world that belongs to God.

Susan M. Felch
Executive Editor
The Calvin Press

Additional Resources

In 2017, Pennylyn Dykstra-Pruim and Tim Baldwin gathered together a number of faculty, students, and alumni of Calvin University and Calvin Theological Seminary to form the Refugee and Immigration Collaborative. The collaborative met periodically over the course of a year to study, discuss, and produce resources that would help Christians think about the issue of immigration from the perspective of faith. Among the resources the collaborative produced are a website (https://ri-collaborative.org/) with stories, short videos, and other helpful material and two companion volumes on immigration in the Calvin Shorts series:

> *Immigrants, the Bible, and You* by Amanda W.
> Benckhuysen
> *Immigration Debates in America* by William Katerberg

For those who seek to grow in their understanding of biblical perspectives, history, and current realities of immigration, we offer the fruit of our participation in the collaborative as a good place to start.

Additional online resources for *Immigration Debates in America*, including discussion questions, are available at www.calvin.edu/press. References and citations are included in the notes at the end of this book. Rather than using footnote numbers, the comments are keyed to phrases and page numbers.

Immigration Debates in America is underwritten
by the Calvin Center for Christian Scholarship
and the Mellema Program in Western
American Studies.

Acknowledgments

The inspiration for this book was the Refugee and Immigration Collaborative at Calvin University. My thanks to Pennylyn Dykstra-Pruim and Tim Baldwin for asking me to participate in the collaborative. And thanks to my fellow participants for helping me understand what aspects of the history of immigration are most important from the viewpoint of present-day concerns.

I am grateful for Calvin University resources that went into this project. The Calvin Center for Christian Scholarship and the Calvin Alumni Association cosponsored the collaborative. And the Mellema Program in Western American Studies helped to support the publication of this book.

My thanks also to people who helped in hands-on ways with the book. Susan Felch and Michaela Osborne at the Calvin Press were essential to the project. Susan helped me to think about my audience for the book and to clarify aspects of the story it tells. Michaela helped with designing the book and material to promote it.

One of the things I have learned over the years is that "my" best ideas are rarely my own in any simple way. They are a product of thinking through things I have read and of conversations with other scholars, students, and public audiences. Several colleagues discussed ideas for this book with me or gave me feedback on portions of the book. Special thanks to John Fea and Kristin Du Mez for their feedback on the whole manuscript.

My hope is that readers will see immigration and immigration debates in American history in some new ways. I also hope that as a result they will see themselves and their communities today in new ways, whether they and their families have lived in the United States for many generations or have recent immigrant experience.

Within
These Gates

1

The United States has long been a country of immigrants. Indeed, except for those of Native American ancestry, every US citizen traces her or his story to an immigrant family.

For just as long, there have been debates about immigration. The goal of this book is to step back and look at these debates. We will focus on six moments of debate about immigration. When we look at these debates, we can see ourselves in a distant mirror of sorts. We can learn something about ourselves as we examine our ancestors and their values. And we can think about what our religious and political values call us to do today.

Consider this story. In 1835, Samuel Morse, a painter and inventor who soon would develop the telegraph and Morse code, feared that thousands of unfit people were pouring into his country every day. He wrote a book called *Foreign Conspiracy Against the Liberties of the United States* to alert Americans to the danger. "Our institutions," he claimed, "are at the mercy of a body of foreigners. . . . We are the dupes of our own hospitality." Some applauded him. Others were appalled. When he ran for mayor of New York City, he came in fourth of four, receiving fewer than fifteen hundred votes.

Despite his defeat, Morse spoke aloud the sentiments of many other Americans. He worried that these foreigners threatened American freedom. He thought that they would not, and could not, adopt American ways. Not all of them are dangerous, he admitted, but enough are that we must "suspect them all." The government should bar them from coming to America.

Who were the terrible and unfit immigrants feared by Morse? They were German Roman Catholics. Like many other native-born, Protestant Americans, Morse also worried about Irish Roman Catholics.

Fear of Roman Catholic immigrants in the 1830s turned American politics upside down. Anti-Catholics made up stories about conspiracies in Roman Catholic

RIOT IN PHILADELPHIA
JUNE 7. 844.

H. Bucholzer, "Riot in Philadelphia," July 7, 1844. Lithograph. In Philadelphia in May 1844, Protestant rioters burned two Roman Catholic churches after the bishop persuaded school officials to use the Latin Vulgate Bible as well as the King James Bible in local public schools. Rioting in July 1844 required the state militia to restore order. *Library of Congress LC-USZ62-3536.*

convents and schools. Their claims sometimes inspired violence. In 1834, a mob burned down a convent in Massachusetts, destroying Bibles and musical instruments and stealing communion wafers as they joked, "Now I have God's body in my pocket."

IMPORTANT CONCEPTS

Historians call this kind of opposition to immigration "nativism." They mean campaigns by "native-born" Americans to keep the wrong kinds of immigrants from coming to the United States. Morse ran for mayor on a nativist platform. In his day, the unwanted immigrants were Roman Catholic and Irish and German. Acceptable immigrants were Protestant and from Britain and northwestern Europe. For nativists, democracy depended on attracting the right kinds of immigrants, assimilating them to American life, and keeping out the wrong kinds.

Debates about immigration have shaped the United States since its origins. These debates are closely tied to two types of nationalism that scholars call "ethnocultural" and "civic." These are ideal types. Some people fit them closely. Others fall somewhere in between.

Nativists like Morse have promoted an "ethnocultural" vision of America. They believe that ethnicity, race, culture, and religion, not just political values like freedom and rule of law, are essential to the nation and citizenship. Until World War II, this viewpoint generally meant that "real" Americans were white, Anglo-Saxon, and Protestant. "Anglo-Saxon" referred to people from the British Isles (but not the Irish) and northwestern Europe.

In this vision, you are born into a nation. You can't choose to be white or English, Swedish, or Scottish, if you were born black or Irish, German, or Chinese. Religious tradition, ethnic and racial background, and political values come as a package. Protestants in countries like England and the Netherlands established the values of freedom and habits of self-government. Democratic government is incompatible with being Roman Catholic, where you must bow to the pope's authority. And people from the wrong kinds of ethnic and racial groups are morally corrupt, biologically unfit, and not ready for freedom. They might be able to evolve and assimilate in small numbers. But nativists were skeptical.

Americans today generally view ethnicity and race as separate categories. Ethnicity focuses on cultural heritage, such as English, French, Korean, or Japanese. Race usually focuses on outward appearance, especially skin color. In the 1800s and early 1900s, people often referred to ethnic groups like the Irish as distinct "races." They ranked "races" from more advanced to primitive and degraded: whites above blacks, and English and Swedish above Irish, Italian, and Jewish. Politics, religion, and race could not be separated.

Defenders of immigration typically have promoted a "civic" vision of the nation. They also have been pragmatic, emphasizing the need for immigrants as laborers in a growing economy. In the "civic" vision, being loyal to the United States and loving liberty, equality, and democracy are enough to make you American. A person's race or religion does not matter. A civic nation is not something you are born into. It is something you choose, whether you are native-born or an immigrant. The values and habits of freedom are not tied to specific racial, ethnic, and religious backgrounds. Self-government may have emerged first in places like the Netherlands and England, but it is not inherently Protestant, English, or Dutch. Catholics, Muslims, Buddhists, and atheists can be loyal Americans too. And no ethnic or racial group is unfit for self-government. Immigrants can adapt to American life, and they should be welcome.

Archbishop John Ireland of Minnesota expressed this civic vision in 1903, saying, "The vital principle of democracy must ever animate the Republic. Every man must be equal before the law with every other man in civil and political rights. It matters not what his place of birth, his religious creed, his race or color, if he is an American citizen, the laws of the land must shield him, the favors of the land must flow upon him." Ireland was Roman Catholic and an immigrant, his family having fled famine in Ireland in 1848. He was a man of his time in being hesitant to support the right of women to vote and hold office. But he was forthright about rejecting ethnicity, race, and religious background as essential to American liberty and citizenship. He defended the rights of African Americans.

He urged immigrants to embrace American life. And he insisted that being Roman Catholic was no bar to being a loyal American.

OUTLINE OF THE BOOK

This book tells the story of the debates about immigration in American history. It focuses on people who worried about immigration, because they set the agenda for these debates in the nineteenth and early twentieth centuries. It sets their fears within the larger history of conflict over the kind of nation we should be. Opponents of immigration were not tied exclusively to a particular political party. They came from political parties that many Americans have forgotten, such as the Whig, Native American, Populist, and Progressive parties. And they have been members of the Republican and Democratic parties. All, however, worried about the ways that immigrants might change the life and culture of the United States. Defenders of immigrants, similarly, came from across the political spectrum.

Debates about immigration are part of a larger story about whether all people born in the United States should enjoy full citizenship and be treated equally. This story includes slavery, abolition, and equality for African Americans. It includes the conquest of Native peoples, the first nations of the Americas. And it includes the annexation of Texas (1845), the Mexican-American War (1846–48), and one hundred thousand Mexicans becoming part of the United States. Finally, the story of the nation is about gender. The United States denied women full citizenship until 1920. The idea of equality in the early 1800s assumed that only people who were the same could be equal. Could people who in some way were different be full citizens? This book focuses on debates about immigration, but it makes connections to this larger story.

This book begins, in chapter 2, with Morse's era and campaigns against Irish-Catholic immigration, emphasizing religious sources of anti-immigrant sentiment. Chapter 3 turns to anti-Chinese legislation and opposition to Asian immigrants more broadly (1850s–1920s). Chapter 4 examines immigration policies about Europeans (1880s–1920s) and the use of "national origins" quotas to preserve the ethnic and religious makeup of the United States. Chapter 5 explores the rejection of Jewish refugees from Hitler's Germany and describes the evolution of refugee and immigration policies after World War II. Chapter 6 puts today's debates about immigration from Mexico and Central America in the context of the long history of the Mexico-US borderland region. Chapter 7 returns to religious concerns, examining the history of Muslim Americans and debates about Muslim immigration today. Finally, chapter 8 reflects on what we can learn from this history if we use it as a mirror to examine ourselves and debates today.

Opposition
to Irish
Catholics

2

Irish-Catholic immigrants to the United States were a success story in 1900. Most came as poor, unskilled manual laborers. Their American-born sons worked as skilled laborers, clerks, and police. Some ran labor unions, went to college, and became lawyers and doctors. A few owned large businesses and won influence in politics. Their daughters became secretaries, nurses, and schoolteachers.

An ordinary example is the Poughkeepsie, New York, family of John Kearney. He came as a "famine Irish" immigrant before the Civil War. Kearney first worked as a manual laborer. He later opened a junk dealership and bought a small house. His oldest son started as a grocery clerk and eventually became inspector of Poughkeepsie's waterworks. Another son started as a clerk in the post office and rose to superintendent of the city streets.

Second- and third-generation Irish Americans who climbed into the middle class sometimes were called "lace curtain" Irish, in contrast to their "shanty" Irish parents. They owned homes with plush carpets, fancy furniture, and nice silverware. Their respectability reduced the fears of native-born Americans who opposed Irish immigration, even if they still frowned on Catholicism. But why were so many native-born Americans afraid of Irish-Catholic immigrants in the first place?

To answer this question, this chapter explores anti-immigrant campaigns before the Civil War (1861–65). Nativism in this era focused on Roman Catholic, Irish, and German immigrants. Some 4.8 million people emigrated from Britain and Europe to the United States from 1830 to 1860. They included 1.5 million German and 1.9 million Irish newcomers. Some fled poverty, famine, and political oppression at home. Others sought opportunity in the United States, with its growing economy and land to farm. Social changes in the United States intensified concerns about immigrants. These changes included the start of an industrial economy and the steady growth of towns and cities. They also included boom-and-bust cycles in the economy.

Opposition to immigration was part of a larger set of responses to these social changes. It complemented religious revivals and moral reform campaigns meant to keep American society from growing unstable and corrupt in an era of change. It also was connected to conflicts between the North and the South over slavery and the growth of religious groups such as Mormons. Many Americans in this era hoped to see the kingdom of God in America. They believed that if they failed to promote godly freedom, the Almighty might condemn America and bring destruction to it, as with ancient Judah and Israel.

ANTI-CATHOLICISM

"Popery is a *Political system*, despotic in its organization, *anti-democratic* and *anti-republican*, and cannot therefore coexist with American republicanism," Samuel Morse claimed in 1835. What did people like him mean when they said these things about Roman Catholics?

Anti-Catholics claimed that the Roman Catholic Church was not a true church and religion. They saw it as a foreign political power. They believed that Catholics obeyed their leaders like slaves. Catholics were loyal to a foreign power, their church, not to the United States. The church opposed freedom and democracy. Catholics would vote as the church commanded them. Catholics thus would control American politics and subvert democracy. They could not be trusted as citizens and were unworthy of freedom.

Anti-Catholic sentiment had deep religious roots. Protestants often said that the pope was the antichrist and that the Roman Catholic Church was a tool of the devil. They remembered centuries of religious wars between Protestant and Roman Catholic nations and martyrs killed by the Catholic Church. (Catholics, of course, had their own martyrs, killed by Protestant rulers.) Many Americans believed that God had called the United States to be a beacon of Christian freedom and democracy. The "Romish" superstitions of Catholic immigrants threatened American freedom, true Christianity, and the growth of the kingdom of God in the United States.

Such sentiments could be found among some of the founders of the new nation, notably John Adams, its second president. His successor, Thomas Jefferson, rejected such views, defending the freedoms not just of Catholics but of Jews and Muslims too.

There were half-truths in what anti-Catholics said. Some Catholics in America and Europe dismissed Protestant Christianity as the work of the devil, insisting that salvation came only through Rome. Popes often criticized democracy during the nineteenth century. Catholic leaders viewed religious freedom as dangerous. How could true Christians support freedom of religion for heresy and faithlessness?

What Protestants usually did not acknowledge was their own fear of religious freedom. They supported religious freedom for believers like themselves, but less so for others, such as Catholics and Jews. Baptists and Methodists had suffered persecution in Britain and its North American colonies in the 1700s. Now they enjoyed freedom and influence but were reluctant to support the same for new religious minorities.

RACIAL AND SOCIAL FEARS

Opponents of immigration also viewed immigrants as morally and racially dangerous, especially the Irish. One concern was their sheer number. The percentage of foreign-born people in the United States rose from under 2 percent in 1830 to over 13 percent in 1860. The Irish fled poverty and a long history of oppressive British rule. Famine in 1845 led to an exodus, with impoverished immigrants leaving Ireland for Britain, Canada, and the

United States. So many left or died of starvation, malnutrition, or disease that the population of Ireland fell from 8.2 million in 1841 to 5.8 million in 1861.

Thomas Nast, "The Ignorant Vote," cartoon in *Harper's Weekly*, December 9, 1876. The cartoon depicts the Irish as racially unfit for democracy, like freed African Americans in the post–Civil War South. Neither "race" was ready for freedom, many Americans believed. Both were depicted as ape-like or monsters and as threats to white women. The cartoon also reveals how nativism related to racism against African Americans. *Library of Congress LC-USZ62.*

Most Irish immigrants came to the United States as single men and women. Most settled in American towns and cities, looking for work. The men toiled in factories, dug canals, and worked the railroads. The women worked in factories too. They also served as maids and cooks in wealthy homes. Irish immigrants generally lived in the poorest neighborhoods, areas plagued by sewage, dirty water, and poorly ventilated buildings. They died from cholera and typhus, sometimes carrying these diseases from Ireland, sometimes catching them in North America. Nativists viewed these health issues as a sign of racial and moral weakness, overlooking how poverty and living conditions caused epidemics among the Irish. They viewed the Irish as a lesser race, not really "white," and often compared them to African Americans.

Protestant Americans also associated Irish immigrants with alcohol, drunkenness, violence, and sexual immorality. They feared that immigrants would corrupt the thousands of young native-born Protestant American women and men seeking work in towns and cities.

The growth of towns and cities combined with mass immigration to spur fears about the fate of democracy in America. The northeastern states were the most urban in the nation in 1820, at about 11 percent. By 1860, the urban population had risen to 36 percent. Americans believed that without a strong moral order, a free society would fall into corruption and chaos. What would happen as millions of young women and men moved from farms to cities looking for work? They would be living without families and familiar communities and churches to watch over them. Would the immigrants pouring into the same cities cause further temptation, with drink, dancing, and illicit sex? The participation of immigrants in labor unions and strikes was a concern too. Did immigrants bring radical, un-American political ideas with them?

MORAL AND POLITICAL CAMPAIGNS

To counter the dangers they feared, social reformers started moral reform campaigns. Chief among these campaigns was "temperance," which encouraged people to drink less alcohol or to give it up altogether. Women activists played a leading role in temperance campaigns. Their role reflected assumptions about women's naturally pious and moral nature. But their activism also led some women to promote women's right to vote and hold office. Church leaders promoted Sunday schools and religious revivals. They hoped that young people would follow the Holy Spirit to the house of the Lord rather than go to taverns and brothels. Business leaders financed these moral campaigns and religious revivals. They hoped to promote democracy and God's kingdom in America. They wanted employees ready to work in the morning, with clear heads rather than hangovers. Following Jesus also might keep workers from joining labor unions.

Irish Catholics were targets of all these campaigns. Employers favored immigration, typically, needing more cheap laborers. If the Irish could not be kept out of the United States, and if they were needed as workers, perhaps they could be reformed.

Moral campaigns and opposition to immigration overlapped with the other major issue of the time: slavery. Reformers and critics of immigrants tended to be anti-slavery. For some, this meant preventing the spread of slavery into the frontier territories of the West. For others, it meant abolishing slavery wherever it was, including the South. Slavery was a sin and incompatible with liberty. God would punish the United States if it did not abolish slavery. Slaveholders in the South were skeptical of anti-immigrant campaigns. This was not because they cared about immigrants. It was because they associated reform movements and anti-immigrant campaigns with opposition to slavery. They worried that reform movements threatened their right to own slaves and spread slavery in places like Arkansas and Kansas.

The Mexican-American War of 1846 to 1848 is another example of the overlap between opposition to slavery and opposition to immigration. Texas won independence from Mexico in 1836. The United States rejected making Texas an American state at that time because states in the North did not want to add another slave state to the nation. Opponents of slavery and immigration also opposed the war and incorporating territory won from Mexico into the United States—what is now California, Nevada, Utah, Arizona, New Mexico, and parts of Colorado, Kansas, Oklahoma, and Wyoming. The new territory threatened to allow slavery to spread, and it would bring tens of thousands of Roman Catholic Mexicans into the nation. Irish and other Catholic immigrants fought in the American armies that invaded Mexico. Some of them deserted the US Army when they saw Protestant soldiers vandalize Catholic churches. The anti-Catholicism that the Irish experienced in the United States gave them sympathy for Mexican Catholics.

Conflicts over immigration and slavery transformed American politics. In the 1820s, the Democratic and Whig

Parties dominated American politics. In the 1840s and 1850s, new parties emerged. The Native American Party campaigned against Irish Catholics and other immigrants. Its supporters were dubbed "Know Nothings" because members of nativist societies supposedly claimed to know nothing about their organizations. The Free Soil Party opposed the spread of slavery into new frontier territories. Together, the two new parties broke the Whig Party. In the 1850s, the new Republican Party gathered together voters concerned about immigration and opposed to slavery. The Democratic Party attracted immigrant voters in the North and supporters of slavery in the South.

ANTI-CATHOLIC LEGACIES IN THE TWENTIETH CENTURY

Fear of Irish immigrants declined in the late nineteenth century. By the 1890s, the Irish (and Germans) were "old immigrants," familiar in the United States. Many had worked their way into the middle class and become influential in politics. They had proved their loyalty in the Civil War. The Democratic Party continued to win support from immigrants and from whites in the South. Some immigrants became Republicans (especially Protestant ones). Still, the party was more associated with anti-immigrant sentiment. Nativists had come to fear "new immigrants" from eastern and southern Europe— Poles, Jews, Italians, Russians, and Greeks, for example (see chap. 4). Anti-Catholicism continued to shape American politics, as many of the new immigrants were Roman Catholic.

A good example of this anti-Catholicism is the second wave of the Ku Klux Klan in the 1910s and 1920s. The "second Klan" was bipartisan, including both Democrats and Republicans. It continued to promote white supremacy in the South. But it focused on the "new immigrants," Catholics and Jews, more than African Americans. It grew in the Midwest and the West more than in the South. It was larger in towns and cities, such as Detroit, than in the countryside. As many as 5 million Americans had joined the Klan by the mid-1920s. Thousands of Protestant clergy joined the Klan too, though others, across the country, condemned the Klan.

The second Klan defended a moral order that it associated with Protestant Christianity. Members feared the new modern, urban era associated with the Jazz Age. They believed that foreign races and religious traditions would only worsen moral decline. In 1928, the Democratic Party nominated Al Smith, a Roman Catholic from New York, for president. Anti-Catholic animus helped defeat Smith. But his nomination was a turning point, or at least the beginning of one.

John F. Kennedy was the next Roman Catholic nominated for president, in 1960. He won a narrow victory, defeating Richard Nixon, a Quaker. The United States had made a significant turn in the thirty-two years since Al

Smith's defeat. Catholics had fought in the US military during World War II. The Holocaust had undermined the respectability of racial and religious prejudices. By the 1950s, Americans were talking about the country as a Judeo-Christian nation. Civil rights campaigns for African Americans and other racial minorities were changing the nation too. Old fears died hard, however.

Kennedy had to calm the doubts of nervous Protestant clergy. He promised them, "I believe in an America where the separation of church and state is absolute, where no Catholic prelate would tell the president (should he be Catholic) how to act." Kennedy added pointedly, "And no Protestant minister would tell his parishioners for whom to vote," and "no man" would be "denied public office merely because his religion differs from the president who might appoint him or the people who might elect him."

Anti-Asian Legislation

3

Chung Sun arrived in Los Angeles with $600 in 1871. He had dreams of starting a tea plantation. Mob violence and racist policies soon turned him bitter. A riot broke out in Los Angeles in October 1871. White workers hung, stabbed, and shot Chinese workers, killing twenty-three. Police sent to stop the violence encouraged it instead. Rioters beat Chung Sun and robbed him. He survived only because he could speak enough English to convince them not to kill him.

Chung left for Santa Cruz County soon after the riot, where he found a job digging ditches. There he became friends with C. O. Cummings, editor of a local newspaper, the *Watsonville Pajaronian*. Cummings published a series of letters by Chung in November 1871. "I hope you will pardon my expressing a painful disappointment," Chung said sadly. "The ill treatment of [my] countrymen may perhaps be excused on the grounds of race, color, language and religion, but such prejudice can only prevail among the ignorant." "In civility, complaisance, and polite manners," he concluded, Americans "are very properly styled barbarians."

Mob violence was not the only problem that Chinese immigrants like Chung faced. Laws in California had made it difficult for him to find work. In 1882, a new federal law would bar Chinese immigration. He had left China to find freedom and opportunity in the United States. He found nothing but hardship. He scraped together enough money to buy passage across the Pacific and went back to China.

This chapter explores opposition to Asian immigrants. Nativists like Samuel Morse failed to ban Roman Catholic immigrants in the 1830s to 1850s. Anti-Chinese campaigns succeeded in the 1880s. Their success started a system of racist immigration policies and institutions that culminated in the 1920s with all Asian immigration banned and strict quotas for European immigrants (see chap. 4). Anti-Asian movements also help us to see how opposition to immigrants related to foreign policy and to policies against minority groups in the United States.

THE GOLD RUSH AND ANTI-CHINESE CAMPAIGNS

The gold rush in California drew tens of thousands of Chinese in the 1850s, over twenty thousand in 1852 alone. It also drew people from across the United States and from Canada, Latin America, and Europe. Chinese immigrants called California "Gold Mountain." They spread along the Pacific Coast and in the mountain West over the next three decades. They worked in mines, on railroads, and in laundries, restaurants, stores, and hotels. Hundreds of Chinese women also came to the region, some taken from China by kidnappers, many sold into indentured servitude by their penniless families. They worked in laundries, restaurants, and hotels or as prostitutes. Millions of Chinese also emigrated in the 1800s and early 1900s to southeast Asia, western Canada, South America, Hawaii, and Australia. They fled civil war in China, as the Qing Dynasty declined and Britain, European powers, the United States, and Japan took control of China's economy.

J. Keppler, "A Picture for Employers," cartoon in Puck, August 21, 1876. The cartoon depicts the Chinese as living like animals in a filthy crowded room, taking opium, and eating rats. It contrasts them to a virtuous American man arriving home from work to wife, children, and normal household conditions. This explains why Chinese workers can "live on 40 cents a day" and American workers cannot, the cartoon states. *Library of Congress LC-USZ62-57340.*

From the start, Chinese immigrants faced prejudice and brutal discrimination in California and the wider nation. As nonwhites, they were ineligible to become naturalized citizens. Whites spoke fearfully of a "yellow peril." They viewed the Chinese as a threat to the white race and Christian civilization. Cities created segregated "Chinatowns." In mining regions, the Chinese lived in separate camps. In 1855, California imposed a "head tax" of $50 on every Chinese immigrant to the state. The state supreme court ruled this tax unconstitutional. The state legislature kept trying new head taxes and banning Chinese immigration, and courts kept ruling the laws unconstitutional.

Violence against Chinese immigrants became common in California and the mountain West as their numbers grew. Mobs in San Francisco and Los Angeles burned their homes and stores. They cut off the "queues" (braided hair) of Chinese men and lynched, branded, scalped, and castrated them. Most white Americans viewed the Chinese as immoral, lazy, dirty, diseased, and drug addicted. At the same time, white laborers hated the Chinese for taking "their" jobs. European immigrants like the Irish, who suffered their own discrimination, were as hostile as native-born Americans.

Racism against Chinese immigrants united conservatives and progressives, Democrats and Republicans. Most labor unions refused to allow Chinese or other nonwhite workers to join. Radical unions such as the Knights of Labor and International Workers of the World sometimes were an exception. Employers exploited racism to divide workers against one another. They succeeded.

An example is the massacre of Chinese workers in Rock Springs, Wyoming, in 1885. The Union Pacific Coal Department paid Chinese miners less than white miners. White miners believed that employers used Chinese workers to keep wages low and preferred Chinese over white laborers for that reason. A mob of white miners, most of them immigrants, attacked and killed twenty-eight Chinese men. They wounded fifteen more, burned homes, and caused $150,000 in property damage. Most of the white miners were part of the Knights of Labor. The national organization had opposed anti-Chinese legislation and tried to organize nonwhite workers. But racism and employer policies of paying nonwhites lower wages led members of the Knights in the West to promote Chinese exclusion.

Irish immigrants often joined in too, their own experience of bigotry notwithstanding. They wanted to rise in the American racial hierarchy and be accepted as "white." Denis Kearney, a labor leader born in Ireland, led the charge to exclude Chinese immigrants. He founded the Workingmen's Party of California in 1877. He attacked businessmen for exploiting workers but spared no sympathy for Chinese workers. His speeches ended with the slogan "The Chinese must go." "If the ballot fails," he would proclaim, "we are ready to use the bullet." Kearney traveled the country to make his case. The Workingmen's Party won enough seats in the California State Assembly and Senate in 1878 to pass a law denying Chinese the right to vote in California.

NATIONAL POLICIES

The United States made discrimination against Chinese immigration national policy in the 1870s and 1880s. In 1875, it excluded Chinese women. The Chinese Exclusion Act of 1882 suspended all immigration from China for ten years. The United States renewed the policy in 1892 and made it permanent in 1902. These policies were the start not just of anti-Asian legislation but also of federal laws to regulate immigration generally.

The new laws sometimes targeted racial groups directly, but until the 1920s, they mostly did so indirectly. Alien Contract Labor laws in the 1880s made it illegal for people to pay the transportation costs of an immigrant as part of a contract to work in the United States. Congress hoped the law would slow the flow of immigrants from Asia and from southern, central, and eastern Europe. Nativists opposed these immigrants on racial grounds. Native-born laborers opposed them as cheap competition for jobs, believing that "lower races" were willing to take lower wages than native-born white workers would accept. In 1903, the United States excluded polygamists and political radicals as immigrants, and in 1907, it excluded unaccompanied children and people with physical or mental defects. Officials often enforced these laws selectively, depending on the health of the American economy and the race of the immigrants.

A series of laws and agreements in the 1900s targeted Asian immigrants generally. In 1894, the United

States had signed an agreement with Japan allowing the Japanese to immigrate to the United States and have the same rights as US citizens. Americans saw the Japanese as hardworking and intelligent. At the same time, they believed that racial differences meant that the Japanese could never assimilate to American society through inter-marriage. Some American workers and business owners were jealous of Japanese Americans' success as farmers, business owners, and educated professionals. Cities like San Francisco decided to segregate Japanese children with Chinese children in schools.

In 1907, the United States reached a "Gentlemen's Agreement" with Japan. The federal government pressured San Francisco to change its policies, and Japan agreed to restrict emigration to the United States. In 1913, California limited the rights of immigrants not eligible for citizen-ship (i.e., Asians, as nonwhites), denying them the right to own farmland or lease it long term. Their children, born in the United States and thus citizens, could own land. The Immigration Act of 1917 imposed literacy tests on all immigrants and barred immigration from Asia and the Pacific region. The Immigration Act of 1924 confirmed Asian exclusion and added restrictive quotas on European immigrants. These laws sparked outrage in Japan and help to explain the tensions that led to war between the United States and Japan in 1941. The United States would lock up all Pacific Coast Japanese (many of them US citizens) in "relocation" camps during World War II.

Filipino immigrants provide a final example of opposition to Asians. They started immigrating to Hawaii, California, and other coastal states in the early 1900s. They did this as American nationals from 1898 to 1935. The United States had defeated Spain in a brief war from 1898 to 1899. It took Cuba, Puerto Rico, the Philippines, and a few other colonies from Spain and made them American colonies. It then fought a brutal war with the Filipinos, who were seeking independence, first from Spain and then from the United States. People born in these colonies became US "nationals" (not citizens). Filipinos in the United States worked in agriculture, fishing, and service industries. They become the new "yellow peril" in the 1910s and 1920s. But as US nationals, immigration laws did not apply to them. So in 1935, the United States reached an agreement with the Philippines. The United States granted the Philippines local self-government and promised it full independence in the future. In return, it rescinded "nationals" status for Filipinos.

WHITE DOMINANCE AT HOME AND ABROAD

The story of Asian immigrants is a reminder of the relationship between domestic and foreign issues related to race. White Americans waged four campaigns to secure their racial dominance in the United States during the late 1800s and early 1900s.

First, nativists used vigilante violence and legislation against Asian and southern and eastern European

immigrants. Second, Southerners secured white dominance over freed slaves, defeating post–Civil War efforts
known as "Reconstruction" to secure equality for "freed-
men." "Jim Crow" laws in Southern states denied African
Americans legal equality and the right to vote and run for
office. The Ku Klux Klan and other paramilitary organizations lynched and jailed people and burned down homes
and churches to intimidate African Americans and white
allies who asserted black civil rights. Third, the "Indian
Wars," violations of treaty obligations, a system of reservations, boarding schools, and suppression of traditional
religious practices amounted to near genocide against
Native Americans. "The only good Indian is a dead
Indian," some Americans believed. Others argued that
Americans had to "kill the Indian" (culturally) to "save
the man" (as an individual). Finally, vigilantes and local
laws suppressed the civil rights of Mexican Americans
and violated treaties made with Mexico in the wake of the
Mexican-American War of 1846 to 1848.

Campaigns for white dominance at home were tied
to American foreign policy from the 1850s to the 1930s.
The United States joined European powers and Japan in
exercising control of China in the late 1800s and early
1900s. Foreign domination led to decades of civil war, the
collapse of the Qing Dynasty in China in 1912, the victory of communist forces led by Mao Zedong in 1949, and
a flood of refugees. In the 1850s and 1860s, the United
States used the threat of war to force Japan to open itself

to merchants, diplomats, and missionaries. The ruling dynasty collapsed, and Japan fell into civil war. The United States began gobbling up island groups in the Pacific in the mid- to late-1800s, notably the Hawaiian Islands. It celebrated its defeat of Spain in 1899 and the US takeover of Cuba, the Philippines, and Puerto Rico as America's coming of age. The United States now was a global empire like the great powers of Europe. Unlike China, Japan would recover rapidly from its civil war and build modern industry and a modern military. It was an imperial power by 1900 too, competing with the United States for control of the Pacific. This competition culminated in the Japanese attack on Pearl Harbor and the Pacific theatre in World War II.

Opposition to immigration, world-wide expansion, and the story of white dominance at home are connected in three ways. First, the US global empire was an extension of its conquest of frontiers at home, defeating Native American nations and Mexico and taking their land. The United States celebrated white dominance and power—proclaiming America to be an "empire of liberty." Second, American expansion helped to create circumstances that pulled nonwhite groups into the United States, either by conquest or by immigration. Third, the immigration of Europeans and Asians to the United States was part of a global pattern of migration. The United States was the largest attractor of immigrants, but it was not unique. Canada, Brazil, South Africa, Argentina, and Australia also attracted Asian and European immigrants. They also had their own forms of racism and opposition to immigration.

In short, immigration and race relations are part of the story of globalization in the modern era. Nativists often were enthusiastic proponents of expansion abroad. But they wanted to limit the impact of this globalization at home.

In all these cases, empires asserted that conquest was part of a mission of bringing civilization and Christianity to primitive races. Like children and women, these races were not ready for freedom. They needed to be under the father-like authority of advanced peoples such as white, Protestant Americans. The United States could not afford to give full equality and freedom to domestic minorities such as African, Native, and Mexican Americans. It also could not accept large numbers of Asian immigrants and the wrong kind of European immigrants. In time, perhaps, such groups might be fit for freedom. But not yet.

RARE SYMPATHIES

Americans occasionally had sympathy for Asian immigrants and defended their rights. Judge William Barbour was one of them. Barbour presided over the trial of George Hall in California. In August 1853 in Nevada County, Hall shot and killed a Chinese immigrant named Ling Sing. Hall and his companions had tried to rob Ling Sing and another Chinese man. The jury found Hall guilty but acquitted his friends.

In pronouncing a death sentence on Hall in October 1853, Barbour told him to seek forgiveness from God before he met his maker. "It is repentance, true and sincere repentance alone, [that] can entitle you to his mercy." "Life is the immediate gift of God," Barbour explained, "[and] the right to enjoy this sacred and divine donation must ever remain inviable with a free and well-governed people." The laws of society and the right to "life, liberty, and property" belonged to a Chinese man as much as to American-born white men.

A year later the California Supreme Court overturned the conviction. Chief Justice Hugh C. Murray wrote the opinion. He wrote that, like Native Americans, Chinese could not testify in court against whites. To allow this would be to admit them equal rights of citizenship. Soon they would be voting and holding office, "an actual clear and present danger." The Chinese were "a race of people whom nature marked as inferior," Murray said, "incapable of progress" or "recognizing" American laws.

Racial and
Ethnic Quotas

4

The United States began creating national immigration policies and a federal bureaucracy in the 1880s. The federal governmental had grown significantly to fight the Civil War, and industrial societies like the United States had begun to regulate more areas of life as their economies became national and global in scope. The catalyst for federal immigration policies was agitation against Chinese, Jewish, and southern and eastern European immigrants. The new immigration regime culminated in the National Origins Act of 1924. The goal was to preserve the ethnic, racial, and religious makeup of the United States. At the same time, new civic ideas also gained modest influence—that the United States was a melting pot of immigrants and that cultural pluralism was natural and good.

Native-born Protestant Christians wrestled with what to do in this context. Some advocated harsh restriction policies. Others were cautious optimists. They appealed to the "brotherhood of man." A Baptist minister named Howard Grose is an example. In *Aliens or Americans?* (1906), he asked, "Will we extend the hand of Christian brotherhood and helpfulness to the stranger within our gates?" Grose saw danger in immigrants who were different culturally and religiously, such as Italian Catholics and Russian Jews. The solution, he argued, was programs run by schools, charities, and churches to Americanize and

Christianize immigrants. Immigration restriction also was necessary, to make the number of immigrants manageable enough to allow for assimilation.

"The immigrant comes into a new environment, created alike by civil and religious liberty, and cannot escape its influence," Grose explained. "Freedom is infectious and contagious, and the disease is speedily caught by the old-world arrival." True Christianity (not Roman Catholicism) and Americanization would teach immigrants the right kind of liberty. Grose was hopeful. Nevertheless, he opened his book with the poem "Unguarded Gates" (1892) by Thomas Bailey Aldrich. The poem compared immigrants to wolves who threatened America's gates and to the Goths and Vandals who "trampled Rome."

AMERICAN IMMIGRATION POLICY TO 1880

The federal government did little to regulate immigration before the Civil War. In 1790, it passed a Naturalization Act. The act allowed "free white persons" of "good moral character" to become citizens after living in the United States for two years. In 1795, Congress increased the time to five years. In 1798, fearful of foreign influences from revolutionary France, President John Adams and the Federalists passed the Alien and Sedition Acts. The acts increased the time for naturalization to fourteen years. They also gave the federal government power to deport noncitizens it deemed suspicious or enemies. The government also could deport aliens from hostile nations in time of war. Thomas Jefferson's Democratic-Republicans opposed aspects of these acts. They did not renew the power to deport people in peacetime in 1801. And in the Naturalization Act of 1802, they reduced the time for naturalization to five years.

States also had power to deport immigrants before the Civil War. These powers went back to the colonial era. "Poor laws" allowed colonies to deport transient beggars. States inherited these laws after the American Revolution and used them to deport immigrants. Massachusetts and New York received large numbers of poor Irish immigrants in the 1840s. They implemented immigration laws and created boards of commissioners to deport unwanted immigrants. The laws were about penniless immigrants, but the inspiration was opposition to the Irish. States occasionally deported American citizens of Irish descent, some of them born in the United States, others naturalized citizens.

These laws did not amount to a national immigration policy. First, they were state laws and enforced inconsistently. Second, they did not regulate immigration itself. Nonetheless, state laws and federal naturalization laws provided a basis for a national immigration policy in the decades after the Civil War. Fears of foreign influence also would shape federal immigration policies from the 1880s to the 1920s.

THE "NEW IMMIGRANTS"

In the 1880s Americans viewed Asian and European immigrants as different categories. Most Americans assumed a pecking order of races. Advocates of restriction sought to bar all Asians from the United States but viewed European ethnic groups in gradations of whiteness and racial acceptability. Some could easily adjust to American life. Others threatened to pollute American "blood," morals, and democracy.

"Types and Development of Man," frontispiece to J. W. Buel, ed., *Louisiana and the Fair: An Exposition of the World, Its People, and Their Achievements*, vol. 5 (1905). The image is related to the Louisiana Purchase Exposition, informally known as the St. Louis World Fair of 1904. The image ranks races, with European American groups on top and other groups below. The woman with the torch symbolizes enlightenment in science, culture, and religion. Some readers likely read the image as calling Americans to bring enlightenment to the uncivilized; others would have seen a warning against allowing barbarians into the country.

Immigration boosters wanted immigrants as laborers and farmers in a growing economy. Businesses recruited them to work in a variety of industries, such as mining in the new territories and states of the West. States in the Midwest and on the Plains recruited immigrants to "homestead" farms. Boosters were optimistic about assimilating immigrants or simply more concerned about economic growth than cultural change. They advocated regulating the flow of immigrants and promoted programs to help immigrants adjust to life in the United States. Immigration opponents and boosters agreed that the growth of American cities and the rapid growth of the number of immigrants required moral and social reform.

The United States began building an immigration bureaucracy in the 1880s. Congress gave immigration authority to the Secretary of the Treasury. The United States collected a tax of fifty cents for each immigrant. It barred immigrants with mental illnesses or criminal records and those likely to become "public charges." It forbade contract labor in which recruiters paid the way of immigrants, provided them jobs, and required them to pay off their transportation debt. Charities that helped immigrants adjust to life in the United States felt overwhelmed by the numbers. They began to lobby the government to take more responsibility.

The major reasons for developing modern immigration policy and institutions were the "new immigrants" and labor conflict. In the 1850s, 2.8 million immigrants arrived. Roughly the same number came in the 1860s and the 1870s. Some 5.2 million came in the 1880s, 3.7 million in the 1890s, 8.2 million in the 1900s, and 5.7 million in the 1910s (most of them before World War I began in August 1914). The sources of immigrants steadily shifted from Britain and northwestern Europe to central, southern, and eastern Europe—the largest numbers Italian, Russian, Polish, and German. A growing number were Jewish. The growth of labor unions, strikes, and violence between employers and employees added fears about "foreign" political ideas (e.g., socialism) to fears associated with race and religion.

RACIAL NATIONALISM

In this context, a more consciously racial nationalism grew in the United States. Racial thought and ethnic nationalism were not unique to the United States but common in European countries and settler societies similar to the United States, such as Canada, Australia, and South Africa. "Nation building" required coherent national cultures, not just policies to create strong economies, transportation systems, armies, and navies. The United States needed immigrants as a source of labor in its new industrial economy. This would keep business happy. Nationalists wanted to limit or exclude immigrants who (in their view) did not fit America culturally and politically and thus would be more difficult to assimilate.

People who wanted to restrict immigration could be found across the political spectrum. And they included evangelicals and mainline Protestants. Southerners had been skeptical of federal power to restrict immigration before the Civil War. They now supported race-based restrictions. They saw such restrictions as part of preserving white dominance in the South and the larger nation. Presidents from both parties tended to oppose immigration restriction, as they sought as many votes as possible. In general, Republican legislators nationally and Democrat legislators from the South supported restriction. Democratic legislators in the North sought the votes of immigrant citizens from Europe and opposed strong restrictions. But there was a growing consensus about banning all Asian immigration.

Opponents of immigration in the early 1900s described their ideas using the phrase "race suicide." Native-born Americans, especially the middle class and elite, were having fewer children. Immigrant families tended to have larger numbers. The danger was that "old stock" Americans—white, Anglo-Saxon, and Protestant—would be overwhelmed by the "new immigrants." Such ideas were not fringe. Scholars gave them scientific authority, such as Madison Grant in *The Passing of the Great Race* (1916). Political and religious leaders promoted them, notably President Theodore Roosevelt, Senator Henry Cabot Lodge, and Reverend Josiah Strong. Advocates of "eugenics" wanted to engineer a racially unified nation using racial science, medicine, and government power: Limit racially weak immigrants through immigration restriction. Discourage reproduction by people with physical, mental, or moral defects—for example, through sterilization. And encourage healthy people from the superior "races" to have more children.

Despite opposition, race suicide fears increasingly shaped immigration policy and practices. The Immigration Act of 1891 put control of immigration in the hands of the federal government. The United States began to build immigration facilities to inspect and process immigrants and, when necessary, to hold or deport them. Ellis Island in New York City's harbor is the most famous facility. The United States rejected immigrants who were polygamists or had diseases. Shipping companies made a lot of money recruiting and transporting immigrants. New laws forced them to pay to send rejected immigrants back home.

NATIONAL ORIGINS POLICIES

The new laws did not regulate the national origins of immigrants or consider their readiness to become citizens. Instead, legislators passed larger head taxes and proposed literacy tests to achieve these goals. In the South, selectively applied literacy tests provided an allegedly race-neutral way to bar African Americans from voting. Similar tests could screen out unwanted immigrants. Business leaders who wanted more laborers and principled opponents of restriction opposed such laws. Presidents vetoed them. And some reformers argued that immigrants were not the cause of social ills but their victims.

Raymond O. Evans, "The Americanese Wall, as Congressman Burnett Would Build It," cartoon in *Puck*, March 25, 1916. The cartoon is about a proposed literacy test. Instead of using cannons to defend the wall, Uncle Sam is using pens. The caption says, "You're welcome in—if you can climb it!" *Library of Congress LC-USZ62-52584.*

THE AMERICANESE WALL, AS CONGRESSMAN BURNETT WOULD BUILD IT.
Uncle Sam: You're welcome in—if you can climb it!

In the 1910s and 1920s, campaigns for restriction succeeded. War was the key. The United States fought World War I in the name of freedom. But wartime emotions intensified fears of foreigners. This included Germans, long considered acceptable immigrants. Now Germans were judged a danger to democracy and civilization. In 1917, Congress overrode President Woodrow Wilson's veto to pass an immigration law. The law excluded people who could not read. It excluded all Asians. And it excluded immigrants with radical political ideas. The

Russian Revolution of 1917 had created the Soviet Union. This led to fear of immigrants who were communists and thus a threat to American values. Major strikes in 1919 in the United States and Canada added fuel to the fire. In the "Red Scare" from 1917 to 1920, leaders in both parties supported the deportation of aliens alleged to be radicals.

The result was the Emergency Quota Act of 1921. It was temporary but revolutionary. The act limited European immigration to 3 percent of the number of foreign-born people of each nation as counted in the US Census of 1910. The quotas favored immigrants from Britain and northwestern Europe. They discriminated against southern and eastern Europe. The total allowed was no more than 350,000.

This was still too much for opponents of immigration. The National Origins Act of 1924 reduced the quota to 2 percent and went back to the census of 1890. It favored "old stock" immigrants even more, and it further discriminated against "new immigrants," who had come in large numbers after 1895. It allowed a total of only 165,000 immigrants a year. In 1930, after the start of the Great Depression, President Herbert Hoover ordered officials to further limit immigration.

The new quotas did not apply to immigrants from the Americas. This meant that people from Canada and Mexico did not face the same restrictions, whatever their ethnic-racial background. (See chap. 6 on immigration from Mexico.) Practicality remained a part of American policy. Canadian and Mexican migrants remained available pools of labor when American businesses needed them.

NEW IDEALS

Those who wanted to restrict immigration won the battle to define policy in the 1920s, whatever modest exceptions there were. These policies would hold sway until the 1960s. But new views associated with visions of America as a melting pot of immigrants and the idea of cultural pluralism were emerging in the 1900s, 1910s, and 1920s.

A play called *The Melting Pot* (1908) is an example. Written by Israel Zangwill, a Jewish writer from England, it argued that life in America melted people of diverse origins into a new people, Americans. The idea was not new. It went back to the colonial era. The belief was that something in the American experience transformed people. The freedom of the frontier. Liberty in a democratic society. The absence of age-old traditions. These forces created the "American" and a new nation that included the new immigrants. Rather than a race you were born into, to be an American was to be a product of the nation's environment.

The melting pot idea did not necessarily conflict with the idea of distinct races. It simply asserted that new environments and experiences could overcome such differences and create a new people. Critics of immigration restriction used this idea to express their goals. Social reform programs could turn aliens into Americans, but Americanization required some regulation of immigration. The key was to limit the flow of immigrants to a number that could be assimilated. The melting pot was a progressive idea, for the time, but it was mostly applied to immigrants from Europe. Even pro-immigration reformers usually were skeptical about nonwhites intermarrying and assimilating.

A more radical idea was "cultural pluralism," promoted by philosophers like William James and Horace Kallen (an immigrant), anthropologists like Franz Boas (an immigrant), and journalists like Randolph Bourne. In "Trans-National America," in the *Atlantic Monthly* in 1916, Bourne rejected the melting pot goal of assimilation. He called for a "cosmopolitan America" that accepted immigrants and learned from them. Diversity is what makes the American experiment great, he insisted. Cultural pluralism first caught on among intellectuals. It gradually spread among policy makers, social reformers, and religious leaders sympathetic to immigration. It also shaped the views of civil rights activists who argued for equal rights for African Americans, Mexican Americans, and Native Americans.

The melting pot and cultural pluralism were new ways of making the case for a civic vision of the United States. Those who promoted a racial vision of America won the policy battles in the 1890s to the 1920s. However, fighting World War II and responding to the Nazi Holocaust would inspire a resurgence of the civic vision and would shape policy in the second half of the twentieth century.

Refugee
and Immigration
Policies

5

People have fled persecution, war, and natural disaster throughout world history. The Bible depicts them, as do other ancient texts. And refugees and debates about refugees are a familiar topic in the United States today. To fully understand refugees and policy debates about them today, however, we need to look back to the middle of the twentieth century.

Our ideas about refugees and refugee policies date to the 1930s, 1940s, and 1950s. The context was World War II and the Holocaust. In 1939, amid the Great Depression, the United States turned away Jewish refugees fleeing Nazi Germany. The reaction against the Holocaust and racial thought, and the millions of refugees created by the war, led to new American immigration policies. The new American policies were part of a global regime of human rights ideals and refugee programs created by the United Nations.

JEWISH REFUGEES AND THE *ST. LOUIS*

In May 1939, the ocean liner *St. Louis* left Europe for Cuba. Most of the 937 passengers were Jews fleeing Nazi Germany and other parts of Europe on the eve of World War II. They planned to stay in Cuba only long enough to get to the United States. Most had applied for a US visa, and they had landing certificates from Cuba's director-general of immigration. The media in Cuba and around the world followed the ship as it sailed to Havana, as did the US government and Jewish aid organizations. But opposition to the refugees quickly rose in the Cuban government and press.

Fred L. Packer, "Ashamed!," cartoon in the *New York Daily Mirror*, June 1939. The cartoon shows the *St. Louis* with the words "Jewish refugee ship" coming out of its smokestack. At the base of the Statue of Liberty are the famous words, "Give me your tired, your poor . . . Send those, the homeless, tempest-tossed to me." Hanging from the torch is a sign that says, "Keep Out." Lady Liberty's face is turned away, and the written editorial described her as turning away in shame over America's anti-immigration policy.

In the context of the Great Depression, some Cubans feared that the passengers would take Cuban jobs. These fears combined with anti-Semitism. Nazi agents and right-wing activists in Cuba claimed that the Jews were communists. Some local newspapers were owned by families from Spain who had close ties to the Spanish dictator General Francisco Franco. He had come to power with help from Nazi Germany. When the ship arrived in Cuba, the government accepted twenty-two Jews with US visas in hand and turned the rest away.

The ship left Havana and got close enough to Florida to see Miami's city lights. Passengers sent cables to President Franklin D. Roosevelt, begging him to let them in, and lawyers lobbied the State Department. The United States refused to take "extraordinary measures" to let in the Jewish refugees. They had to "wait their turn" and follow normal immigration procedures, officials said. The United States lobbied Cuba to accept the refugees on "humanitarian grounds" (something the United States itself would not do). Cuba refused.

American public opinion was sympathetic but almost no one advocated letting in the refugees. The reasons were like those in Cuba. The Depression was a factor, and anti-Semitism and nativism remained widespread in America. Millions of people had joined the Ku Klux Klan in the 1920s. Anti-Semitic celebrities such as Charles Lindberg, Henry Ford, and Father Coughlin flourished in the 1930s. Fascist paramilitary groups such as the Silver Shirts, founded by William Dudley Pelley, sprang up, modeled on Hitler's Brown Shirts. In 1940, 1941, and 1942 polls found that one out of five Americans saw Jews as a "menace." In 1942, after the United States had entered World War II, one out of six Americans agreed that Hitler "did the right thing when he took away the power of the Jews in Germany."

In June 1939, after the United States turned the *St. Louis* away, Canada did the same. The ship eventually went back to Europe. Britain took 288 of the passengers. The rest went to countries in Europe. Of these, 87 eventually escaped Europe. About half of those trapped in Europe died in the Holocaust.

From 1933 to 1939, the United States filled its immigration visa quotas for Germany only once, in 1939, leaving backlogs of 75,000 to 200,000 German applicants a year. In 1939, Congress failed to pass a bill that would have allowed 20,000 German refugee children (presumably Jewish) to immigrate to the United States in 1940 to 1941, beyond Germany's quota of 27,370 immigrants. And in 1940, the United States did not fill its German immigration quotas, despite 300,000 applicants.

Hundreds of thousands of Jews tried to flee Germany and Europe in the late 1930s. Countries in Central and South America took tens of thousands. Switzerland took over thirty thousand. Some sixty thousand got to British-controlled Palestine. And tens of thousands went to

China. Only after World War II ended did the United States give priority to "displaced persons" from Europe within its quota system. This allowed about sixteen thousand Jewish DPs to come to the United States.

THE UNITED NATIONS
AND THE POSTWAR REFUGEES

Modern refugee policies emerged at the end of World War II and the beginning of the Cold War. Global upheaval had created over 165 million displaced persons.

World War II and its aftermath displaced 60 million people in Europe. This included the region's remaining Jews. It included millions of ethnic Germans evicted from their homes in Czechoslovakia and Poland. And it included prisoners of war from Eastern Europe and the Soviet Union. Some of those prisoners were trying to get home from Germany, while others were desperate to stay in Western Europe.

The Cold War between communist and capitalist societies also generated refugees, as did the founding of new nations. A million Palestinians fled their homes in 1948 in the new state of Israel during the war it fought with neighboring countries who opposed its creation. The Japanese conquest of China and other parts of East Asia (1938–45) created 90 million displaced persons. Civil war in China after the war and the communist victory in 1949 cause more disruption. The independence of British-controlled India and its division into India and Pakistan in 1947 led to 14 million migrants and refugees (plus 2 million people killed).

Memories of similar events in the recent past inspired policy makers not to fail in the 1940s and 1950s. These events included World War I (1914–18), the Russian Revolution and civil war (1917–21), and Jews fleeing Hitler in the 1930s. People also remembered the failures of the League of Nations, the predecessor to the United Nations. The number of refugees had been much smaller during and after World War I. About 8 million people from different ethnic groups fled fighting between Germany and Russia and targeted campaigns against ethnic minority groups by Russia. The collapse of the Ottoman Empire in 1918 and the creation of Turkey led to refugee crises. Muslims sought sanctuary in Turkey, and Turkey expelled and slaughtered Armenians. The Russian Revolution and the civil war that followed created over a million refugees.

The other crucial legacy of World War I and the Treaty of Versailles was the creation of new nation-states in Europe and the Middle East. President Woodrow Wilson defined America's war aims in 1917 as national self-determination. This meant giving ethnic groups that had lived under the control of empires their independence as nation-states. The war led to the collapse of the Ottoman, Russian, and Austro-Hungarian Empires. In the peace treaty process, the United States, Britain, and France redrew the maps of Europe and the Middle East.

In Europe, they created new nation-states and adjusted the boundaries of some existing ones. In the Middle East, they created "mandate" territories under British and French control. They claimed that Arabs and other ethnic groups in the region were not ready for independence. The people in these territories rightly believed that they were victims of racism and a desire to control the region's oil. They would evolve toward independence during the 1930s and 1940s.

In all these cases, the new nation-states and territories had ethnic and religious minority groups, which often led to political competition and sometimes violent conflict. The relocation of refugees and displaced persons during the interwar years, World War II, and postwar years led to more homogenous nations in Europe. Instability in the Middle East and the vicious ethnic cleansing after the division of Yugoslavia in the 1990s are a reminder that the legacy of the world wars remains with us today.

MODERN REFUGEE AND IMMIGRATION POLICIES

In this broad context, the United States and its allies created the United Nations in 1947. They also implemented an international framework for refugees and other displaced persons. Individual nations who were part of the UN implemented refugee policies internally. The Convention Relating to the Status of Refugees (1951) was a multilateral treaty. The convention defined who refugees are and what their rights are when granted asylum. It originally applied to European refugees from before 1950. In the 1960s the UN began to apply it globally. The convention was meant to protect people outside their country of origin who were unwilling to return home. They did not want to go home because of "well-founded fear of being persecuted for reasons of race, religion, nationality." The convention also laid out detailed obligations for countries like the United States, that signed the treaty. Finally, it created a United Nations High Commissioner for Refugees.

The United States developed its own refugee and immigration policies at the same time. In 1945, President Harry S. Truman ordered the State Department to accept forty thousand refugees. It counted them against annual immigration quotas. The United States began to distinguish refugees from immigrants as a matter of law in the Displaced Persons Act (1948), the Refugee Act (1953), and the Refugee-Escapee Act (1957).

During the Cold War era (1947–89), the United States mostly accepted refugees fleeing communism: Hungarians and Soviet Jews in the 1950s; Cubans after Castro's revolution in the late 1950s and early 1960s and again in the 1980s; Czechoslovakians in 1968; and Vietnamese, Laotians, and Cambodians after the Vietnam War in the 1970s. The United States also took a few thousand Palestinians, fleeing Israeli armies, in the 1940s.

The Immigration and Nationality Act of 1952 included provisions for refugees. It also got rid of obvious racial restrictions. It retained national origins quotas but added small ones for Asian countries. It also changed naturalization policies. This allowed Asian and other nonwhite immigrants to become citizens. The 1952 act emphasized that naturalization required new citizens to be people of good moral character. It eliminated contract labor restrictions. And it gave preference to immigrants with economic potential, skills, and education.

The Immigration and Naturalization Act of 1965 radically revised immigration policy. Congress passed it during the same years as major civil rights legislation. The 1965 act got rid of the race-based national origins quotas that dated to 1924 (see chap. 4). At the same time, however, it added immigration limits for the Americas. These limited for the first time the number of Canadians and Mexicans who could immigrate to the United States (see chap. 6). Like the 1952 act, the 1965 act emphasized economic skills and potential. It maintained limits on immigration by country and in total, but it added exemptions to those limits for family members of immigrants, making the limits on immigration weak.

More than 18 million people immigrated legally to the United States between 1965 and 1995, triple the number that had come between 1935 and 1965. More significant than the number was the dramatic change in the national origins of immigrants. Compared to the past, relatively few people came to the United States from Europe after 1960, as Europe was enjoying a thirty-year economic boom. Immigration from Asia, Africa, the Caribbean, and Latin American increased steadily, aided by provisions for family immigration beyond annual quotas. The 1990 Immigration Act increased the total immigration quota modestly, and it encouraged immigration from "under-represented" countries to increase immigrant diversity. It was a new era, in values and in results.

The new policies, all together, had a dramatic impact on the ethnic and racial makeup of the United States. "In 1965, 84% of Americans were non-Hispanic whites," the Pew Research Center reported. "By 2015, that share had declined to 62%. Meanwhile, the Hispanic share of the US population rose from 4% in 1965 to 18% in 2015. Asians also saw their share rise, from less than 1% in 1965 to 6% in 2015." Without that post-1965 immigration, the United States today would be "75% white, 14% black, 8% Hispanic and less than 1% Asian."

CONCLUSION

The Holocaust undermined the respectability that racial thought had in the United States into the 1920s and 1930s. The Cold War fight for "freedom" against communist dictators also made it difficult to defend inequality and racism. Racism did not disappear, but racist ideology went underground. The thirty years after World War II saw the end of legal segregation and racial immigration policies and the growing influence of the melting pot ideal and cultural pluralism. These changes might have happened without the Holocaust and the Cold War, but probably more slowly and with successful resistance in the name of states' rights.

The impact internationally is also noteworthy. The Holocaust and the Cold War similarly undermined racial justifications for European and American colonies in Asia and Africa. People of color in the United States and in American and European colonies saw civil rights in the United States and independence movements in Asia and Africa as a shared story.

The Mexico-US Borderland

6

In 1953, activists from the American GI Forum warned about an "invasion" from Mexico. The invasion threatened the "health," "economy," and "way of life" of the American people. Their pamphlet—"What Price Wetbacks?"—sounded like nativism. But the forum was a Mexican American group created to fight for public services for Chicano veterans of World War II. Its members had faced discrimination in the military and on returning home. The forum also fought for the civil rights of Mexican Americans. They knew that "wetbacks" was a racial slur against people like them, but their concern was their rights as American citizens. They saw illegal immigrant laborers as a threat. They and many other Mexican American leaders supported Operation Wetback, a campaign to deport undocumented Mexican laborers. Starting in 1954, Operation Wetback broke up families and deported as many as 1.3 million people.

Two decades later, the American GI Forum defended undocumented Mexican immigrants in the United States. It called for rights for migrant workers. And it advocated amnesty for undocumented immigrants. How do we make sense of this change?

Immigration from Mexico to the United States has a distinct history. It involves the migration of people who live next door rather than overseas. A large portion of the United States was Mexican territory (and Spanish before that) until the Texas revolution of the 1830s, the US annexation of Texas in 1845, and the US invasion of Mexico and conquest of northern Mexico in 1846 to 1848.

From the viewpoint of culture, geography, economic relations, and population, the Mexico-US border region has always been artificial. It is a transnational frontier shaped by shared history and border crossing. The border matters, of course. It matters to Mexican Americans. At the same time, to prevent migration across that border is to fight history and geography. It should not be a surprise, then, that the history of immigration policies related to this borderland is complicated.

THE HISTORY OF A BORDERLAND REGION

The American Southwest was shaped by migration and trade long before Europeans arrived. The ancestors of the Aztecs may have migrated from the region into what is now Mexico in the 1100s and 1200s. The ancestors of the Navajo and Apache came from northern Canada to the Southwest a century or so before Columbus. Thousands of years before that, trade brought corn, other agricultural products, ritual items, and religious traditions from Mexico into the Southwest and North America more widely.

The Spanish conquest of Central America and Mexico in the 1500s and 1600s included the Southwest. The northern provinces of New Spain—*El Norte* (The North)—were a buffer zone. This buffer zone protected the heartland

"The Republic of Texas and the United States in 1837," *McConnell's Historical Maps of the United States* (1919). The map shows that much of the territory that became part of the United States was Spanish and then Mexico until the 1830s. The territory that became the Republic of Texas was part of Mexico until 1836. *Library of Congress 2009581130.*

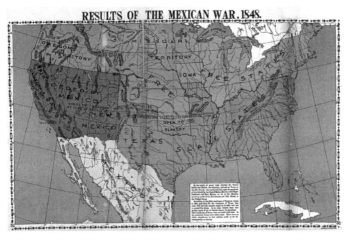

"Results of the Mexican War," *McConnell's Historical Maps of the United States* (1919). In the same period that the United States conquered and annexed northern Mexican, it negotiated a dispute with Britain over the border with British North America (now Canada). *Library of Congress 2009581130.*

of New Spain from powerful Native peoples such as the Comanche and Apache. The Spanish established forts, farming and ranching settlements, and missions to deal with this problem. These in turn fostered small communities made up of *genizaros* ("civilized Indians"), *mestizos* (mixed-blood people), *creolos* (Spaniards born in the New World), and *penninsulares* (Spaniards born in Spain). Native American and Spanish cultural practices blended and mixed, as is common in borderland regions. But these borderland communities failed to help Spain thwart groups like the Apache and Comanche. When Mexico won independence from Spain in 1821, not much changed on the ground in *El Norte*.

In the 1820s, Mexico invited America settlers into *Tejas* (Texas). Mexico's goal was to increase the population and strengthen the region against the Comanche. Anglo-Texans and Spanish-speaking *Tejanos* unhappy with the government in faraway Mexico City rebelled in the 1830s and won independence. The United States chose not to annex Texas in the 1830s due to opposition from anti-slavery states.

In the 1840s, the United States did annex Texas, and it conquered much of northern Mexico. It promised to respect the property rights of Mexicans and to treat them as equal citizens. It did not live up to these promises, however. Mexican Americans became second-class citizens, especially those of mixed-blood and Native descent. Even wealthy Mexican landowners lost much of their land. Control of trade routes shifted from Mexicans to Anglo-Americans. Some Americans called for the United States to conquer all of Mexico in the 1840s, but others opposed this. They did not want to integrate so many nonwhite people into the United States.

The region remained a borderland, however, much like before the American conquest. It was "the West" for Americans, but it remained *El Norte* for Mexicans and Mexican Americans. A similar story could be told about the border region with Canada, with its mix of Native, *Métis* (mixed blood), British, and French peoples.

In the late nineteenth and twentieth centuries, native-born Canadians, Americans, and immigrants crossed the northern border frequently. They wanted land to ranch or farm, hoped to strike it rich in a gold rush, or sought work in mining, timber cutting, or ranching. Labor unions and religious and political movements also crossed the Canada-US border. The big difference from the Southwest was that by 1900 the border crossers in the North mostly were white. Canada developed its own anti-immigrant policies, much like those of the US. It allowed black pioneers from the US, for example, but they faced discrimination and racist campaigns to prevent further black migration.

People of all sorts migrated back and forth across the Mexico-US border in the century after the conquest: Mexicans, Mexican Americans, Native peoples, and white American merchants and laborers. The region remained functionally integrated despite the new international border. The gold rush in California drew over twenty-five thousand Mexican immigrants between 1848 and 1852. Gold seekers also came from all parts of the United States and from Canada, Europe, and China. Mexican Americans hoped to strike it rich too.

Like Chinese immigrants, Mexicans faced discrimination and vigilante violence (with more than 160 Mexicans lynched between 1848 and 1860). More generally, Mexicans and Mexican Americans competed with whites and Chinese for work on farms and as domestics, miners, freight haulers, railroad builders, and cowboys. The cowboy of American frontier mythology is in many ways an import from Mexico.

In 1900, most people of Mexican descent in the United States were native-born. Their communities, from Texas and the Southwest to California, were settled and assimilated, but white-dominated. The next three decades saw significant immigration from Mexico, adding to that from Europe and Asia. In 1900, the population of people of Mexican descent in the United States was five hundred thousand. In 1930, the census counted 1.5 million. When World War I cut off immigration from Europe and put millions of American men in the armed forces, Mexican immigrants became a convenient source of labor in Western states.

Most Mexican immigrants went to the Southwest and California. Smaller numbers went to mountain states, the Plains, and the Midwest. Some were fleeing a revolution and war in Mexico, but most came looking for work. Like European and Chinese immigrants, Mexicans were valued as laborers when needed and faced racist hostility when jobs became scarce. A native-born Mexican American middle class and an elite of business owners and professionals emerged in urban areas. However, most Mexicans and Mexican Americans were poor and working class. They lived in *barrios*, *colonias*, and migrant-worker camps in small towns and rural areas.

Mexican immigrants served as a "reserve army of labor" in the American West during the mid-twentieth century. By the 1920s, the United States had banned Asian immigration and severely restricted immigration from Europe with racially defined annual quotas (see chaps. 3–5). The United States did not restrict immigration from Mexico until the Great Depression, however. In 1932, President Herbert Hoover began a "Mexican Repatriation" campaign. The Immigration and Naturalization Service deported as many as 2 million people. It sometimes caught American citizens of Mexican descent in its sweeps. President Franklin D. Roosevelt ended the campaign in 1933, but some states and cities continued to deport alleged "illegals."

Fears of migrant workers and unemployed people transcended racial boundaries. California set up border stations to check white migrants called "Okies." The Okies were fleeing the Dust Bowl in Oklahoma (and nearby states) and seeking work. Okies with cash could enter California. Police stationed at the state border turned many away others. The difference was the persistence of treating people of Mexican descent as unwanted and denying them full legal rights.

THE *BRACERO* PROGRAM

The entry of the United States into World War II once again meant that it needed Mexicans as laborers. Like other Americans, Mexican Americans moved to cities for work in wartime industries during the war. The war transformed parts of the South and the West into industrial centers, and cities grew dramatically. This growth left rural areas needing workers. In 1942, the United States reached a labor agreement with Mexico. The *bracero* (manual laborer) program brought hundreds of thousands of Mexicans to the United States.

The *braceros* worked on farms and in food-processing plants, especially in Texas, Arizona, and California. The program required employers to pay Mexicans the same as local workers and to reimburse them for their travel expenses. Employers often ignored these rules, however, and the government rarely enforced them. Most migrants lived in foul conditions. Mexicans and Mexican Americans also continued to face legal discrimination and vigilante violence.

A famous example is the "Zoot suit" riot of 1943 in Los Angeles. "Zoot suits" were popular among Mexican American youths. The pants had high waists, baggy legs, and often a chain from a belt loop to a pocket. The coats were long, with padded shoulders. Whites associated the suits with gangs. And white soldiers and sailors resented Mexican American youths who were not in the military. The riot started on June 8, 1943, when a group of sailors and Mexican American youths fought, leaving a sailor wounded. Dozens and eventually thousands of white soldiers and sailors retaliated against Mexican American men (and later African American men). The police largely stood by.

Eventually, the police stopped the rioting with help from vigilante "Vengeance Squads," white rioters among them. They beat Mexican American men for "harassing" white soldiers and sailors. Police arrested hundreds of Mexican American men, but only a few sailors. The local press mostly praised the police and white rioters. The military restricted access to the city by servicemen to prevent further violence.

After the war, the *braceros* were no longer needed. Millions of GIs came home, including Mexican American men, and they needed jobs. Hostility to the *braceros* built up in the early 1950s. Newspapers depicted them not as valuable laborers but as dirty, diseased, and criminal. Mexico cooperated with the United States in Operation Wetback, starting in 1954, because it was experiencing a labor shortage. The United States used military-style operations, packing deportees onto boats and into buses and planes, sometimes sending deportees to unfamiliar parts of Mexico. Many got sick in custody, and some died.

The United States removed as many as 1.3 million people, but the numbers are not clear. Some might have been deported, then returned, and been deported again.

The mix of temporary, permanent, undocumented, and legal migration from Mexico to the United States continued after Operation Wetback. So too did cycles of opposition to it. What changed was the context for immigrants. As we have seen, the United States ended discriminatory immigration quotas with a new law in 1965. And from the 1960s on, most immigrants to the United States were Asian or Latin American. Civil rights campaigns by African Americans and other people of color in the United States began to counter race-based discrimination and violence and to promote pride and power in minority peoples.

Operation Wetback had not ended the b*racero* program. In the late 1950s, the program continued to bring in hundreds of thousands of Mexican laborers. The United States finally ended it in 1964, a year before the new immigration law. The Immigration and Naturalization Act of 1965 ended racist national origins quotas but not quotas. The new law had quotas for every part of the world. For the first time, these quotas included Mexico and the other nations of the Americas. The 1965 act thus restricted legal Mexican and Latin American immigration.

The quotas for Mexico were too low to meet the demand for Mexican labor in the United States. They also were too low to meet the pressures (political conflict and economic problems) that pushed Mexicans to emigrate to the United States. As a result, the flow of Mexicans into the United States did not change, but now many of them came illegally. Between 1969 and 1980, the population of undocumented immigrants in the United States grew from 500,000 to over 2 million. In 1990, it remained about 2 million, but 1.5 million illegal immigrants from other countries added to it. By 2007, there were 6.9 million illegal immigrants from Mexico and 12.2 million in total. The biggest new factor was illegal immigration from Central America, usually through Mexico.

THE CIVIL RIGHTS ERA

Some Mexican Americans opposed illegal immigrants. They valued their familial and cultural ties to Mexico, but they also judged their economic interests to conflict with those of migrant laborers. They believed that their status as American citizens mattered in the competition for jobs. They wanted equal civil rights with other Americans and their rights to jobs and economic opportunities over non-Americans.

Many other Mexican Americans supported migrant Mexican workers, whether legal or undocumented. This support now included the GI Forum, which had advocated deporting migrant workers in the 1950s. It also included Mexican American civil rights organizations and labor unions. Most notably, it included the United Farm

Workers (UFW), led by Cesar Chavez, which organized migrant workers in California.

Labor and civil rights leaders understood that it was impractical to stop people from crossing the border. Civil rights values and a growing interest in their ethnic heritage led Mexican Americans to view their minority status in a new way. It became a matter of pride. Racist campaigns against migrant workers often made no distinction between Mexican Americans and migrants from Mexico. Campaigns against labor unions included racism. Mexican Americans thus came to identify with migrants from Mexico. They also felt sympathy for immigrants from Central America and the Caribbean. In short, most Mexican Americans came to identify with legal and even illegal immigrants. So too did many other Americans who supported civil rights and ethnic pride by minority communities and opposed anti-immigrant policies.

INTO THE PRESENT

The basic patterns of legal and illegal immigration established in the 1960s and 1970s have continued. But they have evolved in noteworthy ways in response to events. For example, the number of undocumented immigrants from Central America has grown since 1980. Immigrants have fled political and gang violence and sought economic opportunity. The flow of immigrants from Mexico and Central America has slowed, even reversed, in bad economic times in the United States and when efforts to deport undocumented immigrants have increased. The recession of 2007 to 2009 is a good example. From a peak of 12.2 million unauthorized immigrants in 2007, there was a net decline to 10.5 million in 2017. These immigrants are part of the larger global migration of people, goods, and money that is shaping the entire planet.

The lines of debate over policy since 1980 have revolved around two sets of issues: border control and immigration. Opponents of Mexican and Central American immigration have focused on preventing illegal border crossings and deporting undocumented immigrants. Advocates for undocumented immigrants have emphasized providing amnesty for those who have been here for a long time, especially those who came as children. They also have proposed increasing the number of legal immigrants and refugees. Some observers have suggested helping governments in Mexico and Central America address problems that push people to emigrate illegally to the United States in the first place.

In the 1980s and 1990s, Republican and Democratic leaders tried to develop practical policies to deal with illegal immigration. Their efforts were bipartisan, and their policies tried to balance control of the border with more legal immigration and amnesty for current illegal immigrants. President Ronald Reagan and a Democratic-led Congress passed the Immigration Reform and Control Act of 1986. President Bill Clinton and a Republican Congress passed the Illegal Immigration Reform and Immigrant Responsibility Act of 1996. It cut legal immigration and significantly increased deportations.

Since the turn of the century, efforts to pass new policy have failed. President George W. Bush and President Barack Obama continued Clinton-era deportation practices. Both tried to develop generous policies for refugees seeking asylum. Bush accepted higher numbers of refugees than in the past, and Obama created an amnesty program known as DACA (Deferred Action for Childhood Arrivals). Bush and Obama also deported record numbers of undocumented immigrants and pushed for bipartisan legislation but failed. The trend from the 1980s to the 2010s was increasing levels of deportation. The number of deportees reached a high under Obama. The shift under President Donald Trump has been to focus deportation efforts not just on felons but on all undocumented immigrants, including targeting families.

Conflicts between Republicans and Democrats have grown more intense during the presidencies of Obama and Trump. Lines of debate that once did not fall along simple party lines increasingly do so. Republicans have focused on deporting most illegal immigrants and reducing the number of immigrants and refugees to the United States in general. President Trump's border wall is a symbol of this. He and his supporters have echoed nativist rhetoric and goals from the past. In turn, Democrats have grown more insistent about amnesty and open borders.

Some seem to oppose any immigration restrictions. These trends have frustrated advocates of compromise in both parties.

Religious responses to the refugee crisis have been complex. A Pew Research poll in 2018 found that 65 percent of religiously unaffiliated people, 63 percent of black Protestants, and 50 percent of Catholics believe that the United States has a responsibility to accept refugees. Only 43 percent of white mainline Protestants and 25 percent of white evangelicals agree. A similar divide exists regarding immigration policies generally. Clearly, race and religion matter in how people view immigrants. For example, Hispanic evangelicals are more likely than white evangelicals to support amnesty for illegal immigrants. But they are less likely to do so than other Hispanics. "God is building his kingdom through the diaspora of people (Acts 17:26)," Y. Liz Dong and Ben Lowe, two evangelicals, wrote, "and we get to join him by welcoming the stranger in our midst." By contrast, Reverend Robert Jeffress, also evangelical, appealed to the Biblical example of Nehemiah rebuilding the wall around Jerusalem to defend the building of a wall along the Mexican border.

These conflicting views reflect the enduring influence of the historic divide between Americans with a more pluralist civic vision of the American nation and those with a more religious and ethnic-racial vision. But the divide is complex and has evolved in subtle ways among religious and ethnic-racial groups. The same trend is evident in responses to Muslim immigrants and refugees today, as chapter 7 suggests.

HISTORICAL PERSPECTIVE

The flow of refugees, especially from Central America, continues to make border control difficult. The integrated nature of the Mexico-US borderland and resistance by advocates for immigrants and refugees in many cities and states have frustrated President Trump's efforts to increase deportations. This should not be a surprise.

The challenge of controlling the Mexico-US border today reflects the long history and geography of the region. The region became "Hispanic" under the rule of Spain and Mexico from the 1500s to the 1800s. But neither could control the region. It has continued to be a "borderland" in the American era, defined by cross-border ties. Demographic trends indicate that the Southwest and larger nation will become more Hispanic over the next few decades. The national border continues to be a cross-cultural borderland as much as a dividing line.

Anti-Muslim
Campaigns

7

Italian Catholics, Dutch Calvinists, and other European immigrants made Paterson, New Jersey, a vibrant blue-collar city a century ago. Muslim immigrants are bringing new life to Paterson today. People refer to one Paterson neighborhood as "Little Ramallah" or "Little Istanbul"—like "Little Italy" and "Chinatown" neighborhoods in the past. The neighborhood has halal butchers, Middle Eastern restaurants, and signs in Arabic. Travel agencies arrange pilgrimages to Mecca, and stores sell fashions to suit ethnic tastes and Muslim modesty. You can find similar enclaves in cities such as Brooklyn, Detroit, and Los Angeles.

Paterson's Arab American mayor, Andre Sayegh, is a devout Roman Catholic married to a Muslim. He is familiar with Americans who wish that Middle Eastern and Muslim immigrants would go "home." He has heard claims that Muslims in Paterson celebrated the terrorist attacks of 9/11. These claims have been debunked. Paterson's Muslim immigrants see the city and the United States as home. It is a place of opportunity and freedom. Crime rates in Paterson's Muslim neighborhoods are lower than in the rest of the city. And interfaith groups are promoting unity among Christian, Jewish, and Muslim residents in the city.

As with Catholic immigrants in the past, debates today about Muslim immigrants are fierce. Anti-Muslim hatred sometimes sparks vandalism of mosques and attacks on individual people. Religious, racial, and ethnic differences get tangled up. And some native-born Americans fear that this new group of people is ill-suited for freedom. This chapter will outline the history of Muslims in the United States and examine debates about Muslim immigrants and refugees.

THE COLONIAL ERA TO THE 1960s

The history of Muslims in the United States goes back to colonial times. About 15 percent of slaves stolen from Africa and taken to Britain's American colonies were Muslims. Some were literate in Arabic and had a rich knowledge of the Quran. Some used this literacy to get better jobs as slaves. All of them struggled to remain Muslim in the absence of a religious community. Some retained or adapted aspects of their traditions; others converted to Christianity. A few eventually became free and wrote autobiographies. An example is Omar ibn Said, a Muslim scholar. He was captured and sold as a slave in the United States in 1807 and wrote his account in Arabic in 1831.

The new American republic recognized the rights of Muslim citizens. A few Muslims of Ottoman Turkish descent fought for the United States in the Revolution. Thomas Jefferson, who had a Quran in his library, included Muslims in his vision of religious freedom. He insisted that the United States recognize "the religious rights of the 'Mahamdan,' the Jew and the 'pagan.'" On the other hand, some critics of the Constitution of 1788 worried that it left room for a Muslim to become president, even if only in the distant future.

A second group of Muslims came from the 1870s to the 1920s. It was part of a larger wave of Arab-speaking immigrants, 90 percent of which was Christian. Muslim or Christian, they went to the Northeast and Midwest. Mohammed Alexander Russell Webb, an American convert, built a mosque and mission in New York in 1898. Another mosque was built in 1893 as an exhibit at the World's Columbian Exhibition in Chicago. The first mosques built by Muslim immigrants date to the 1920s (North Dakota) and 1930s (Iowa and Michigan).

From the 1920s to the 1960s, a small number of African Americans in cities in the North converted to Islam. Some joined orthodox Muslim communities. Others joined African American offshoots such as the Nation of Islam. African Americans make up one-fifth of Muslims in the United States today. Muslims such as Malcolm X played a significant role in the civil rights movements of the 1960s.

THE 1960s TO THE PRESENT

A third and current wave of Muslims began coming to the United States in the 1960s. They come from Africa, the

Middle East, and South Asia (mainly from India, Pakistan, Bangladesh, and Indonesia). Immigrants from these parts of the world who are Christian, Hindu, or Sikh are sometimes confused with Muslims because of their skin color, accents, turbans, or head scarves. Occasionally, this confusion has tragic results. For example, people have confused Sikh Americans with Muslims and attacked them. Today Muslims make up 1 percent of an American population of about 330 million. If current trends continue, in 2050, Muslims will make up 2 percent of a US population of 438 million.

Among Muslim immigrants today are tens of thousands of refugees. Many come from war zones. Some of these war zones involve the United States, such as Iraq and Afghanistan. They also include Syria and a variety of nations in Africa. The United States has averaged about fifty thousand refugees a year since 2000, most coming from Asia and Africa. The number of Christian and Muslim refugees has been about the same on average, with the number of Muslims declining significantly since 2017. Tragic examples of Muslims refused entrance to the United States are those who were promised visas for serving with American forces as interpreters in Iraq and Afghanistan. Some former interpreters have been killed; others have had to flee their homes and have become refugees.

A majority of Americans have opposed accepting refugees since the 1970s. This is true whether refugees were fleeing communism in Vietnam (1970s) and Cuba

(1980s) or violence in the Middle East and Africa (since the 1990s).

The divide on this issue has fallen along religious, racial, and party lines. According to a 2018 Pew Research survey, 68 percent of evangelicals and 68 percent of Republicans say that the United States has no responsibility to accept refugees. By contrast, 74 percent of Democrats, 65 percent of religiously unaffiliated people, and 50 percent of Catholics believe that the United States has a responsibility. White Americans split 48 (no responsibility) to 46 percent (responsibility). Healthy majorities of black and Hispanic voters (67 and 59 percent) emphasize a responsibility. Sixty-one percent of people ages eighteen to twenty-nine emphasize responsibility compared to 43 percent of people over sixty-five, with age groups in between at 51 percent. People with postgraduate (71 percent) and college degrees (63 percent) support responsibility more than those with some college (49 percent) and high school or less education (43 percent).

Muslims arriving since the 1960s have come to an America that has called itself an immigrant nation. Older visions of a white, Anglo-Saxon America (see chap. 4) had mostly disappeared from public life by the 1970s. The public debate was now about "melting pot" versus "multiculturalism." Should the nation aspire to assimilate religious, ethnic, and racial diversity in a melting pot? Or should it welcome multicultural diversity? The line between the two was vague. Was wearing a "Kiss me I'm

Polish" T-shirt and identifying as Polish American melting pot or multicultural? Was promoting ethnic food melting pot but promoting public services in Spanish multicultural? Did integration-oriented civil rights fit with melting pot and "Black Power" with multiculturalism? Did unnoticed storefront mosques in poor neighborhoods signal melting pot while building highly visible mosques in suburban neighborhoods signaled multiculturalism?

IMMIGRATION DEBATES SINCE 9/11

After 9/11, the growing presence of Muslim Americans and fear of terrorists contributed to a revived white Christian nationalism. The goal of this nationalism is to restore a white, Christian America.

President George W. Bush emphasized that the United States was not opposed to Islam. He distinguished ordinary Muslims from radical Islamists, and he visited mosques. Neither the Bush administration (2001–2009) nor that of President Barack Obama (2009–17) proposed immigration policies that discriminated against Muslims. Bush created the Department of Homeland Security (DHS) in response to 9/11. He put the US Customs Service and Immigration and Naturalization Service under the authority of the DHS. Both administrations used these services to safeguard the United States against terrorist attacks.

Conservatives were divided on Islam during the Bush years. Those who supported Bush policies tried to engage

Muslim communities. Other conservatives criticized Bush for his moderation. These critics argued that Islam was incompatible with American values and claimed that all Muslims were a potential danger. They depicted Islam as creating a "clash of civilizations," a war with Christianity and Western civilization. Columnist Ann Coulter was among the loudest. She said in September 2001, "We should invade their countries, kill their leaders and convert them to Christianity."

Donald J. Trump
@realDonaldTrump

We need to be smart, vigilant and tough. We need the courts to give us back our rights. We need the Travel Ban as an extra level of safety!

156K   6:17 PM - Jun 3, 2017

94.9K people are talking about this

Donald J. Trump
@realDonaldTrump

People, the lawyers and the courts can call it whatever they want, but I am calling it what we need and what it is, a TRAVEL BAN!

78K   5:25 AM - Jun 5, 2017

33K people are talking about this

As a candidate and president, Donald Trump has used Twitter to rally support and promote policies. These Tweets from June 2017 defend a travel ban imposed by President Trump's White House on predominantly Muslim countries. Critics labeled it a "Muslim ban."

Coulter's call to kill Muslims might be attributed to the heat of the moment. But her racist rhetoric continued. In 2006, she wrote in a column, "Our motto should be after 9/11: Jihad monkey talks tough; jihad monkey takes the consequences. Sorry, I realize that's offensive. How about 'camel jockey'? What? Now what'd I say? Boy, you tent merchants sure are touchy. Grow up, would you?"

The election of Barack Obama, a Christian whose father had a Muslim background, led to anti-Muslim sentiment becoming increasingly partisan. Obama's policies did not depart in a major way from his Republican predecessor (to the frustration of more progressive Democrats). But without a president like Bush, who reached out to Muslims, the influence of anti-Muslim voices in the Republican Party grew stronger.

Since 2017, President Donald Trump and his Republican supporters have supported anti-Muslim measures as a matter of policy. No new legislation has been passed, but the White House has used enforcement practices to limit visas to Muslims and immigration from Muslim regions of the world. It also has lowered refugee admission goals. Its larger goals have been to reduce the number of legal immigrants and refugees and to remove illegal immigrants. As a candidate and president, Trump has used nativist rhetoric. This rhetoric includes attacks on Ilhan Omar and Rashida Tlaib, the first two Muslim women in Congress. Omar is an immigrant from Somalia; Tlaib is a native-born American from Detroit.

Many Democrats have responded to Republican policies by sounding as if they favor open borders. They have called for amnesty for most current undocumented immigrants and an increase in refugee admission caps. Some support border security and aid to Central American nations to reduce the flows of refugees and immigrants. But they have been reluctant to define goals for immigration levels, whether for immigrants or for refugees. Democratic presidential candidates in 2019 and 2020 said that illegal immigrants should not be deported in the near future, unless they commit crimes. In response to President Trump's efforts to ban or limit Muslim immigration, Democrats proposed a No Ban Act. It would repeal several Trump executive orders and make it illegal to discriminate based on religion.

As with the refugee question, the public is divided along religious, racial, and party lines in their views of Muslims. According to a poll in 2019, fifty-three percent of Jews, 39 percent of Catholics, and 34 percent of nonreligious people have favorable views of Muslims. Thirty-one percent of mainline Protestants and 20 percent of white evangelicals do. Knowing a Muslim person correlates strongly with favorable views of Muslims. Over 75 percent of Jews say they know a Muslim, and 61 percent of Catholics. Only 35 percent of white evangelicals do. Black Americans have more favorable views of Muslims than white Americans. Political affiliation also is a strong predictor of favorable versus unfavorable views of Muslims. A poll in 2015 found that 76 percent of Republicans, compared to 43 percent of

Democrats, believe that "the values of Islam are at odds with American values and way of life."

Immigrant and refugee Muslims have more favorable views of the United States than do native-born Muslim Americans. The favorable views of immigrant Muslims perhaps reflect greater security, opportunity, and freedom in the United States compared to their homelands. Native-born Muslim Americans perhaps experience a gap between American ideals about freedom and equality they are raised with and the treatment of Muslims in the United States they experience and thus are more critical.

Shepard Fairey and Ridwan Adhami, "Greater than Fear." Fairey and other artists created a series of posters as part of the We the People campaign to protest the inauguration of President Trump in 2017. The campaign was promoted through the Amplifier Foundation, a design lab that works with progressive grassroots campaigns. The campaign was meant to "ignite a national dialogue about American identity and values through public art and story sharing." It emphasized racial diversity and inclusion, including in relation to immigration.

CHRISTIAN RESPONSES

Leaders from various Christian groups responded to the Trump administration's efforts to ban Muslim refugees in 2017. Some stated that the ban conflicted with basic Christian values. "It's disappointing to see America's heart closing to refugees," said Richard Stearns, president of World Vision. "This is not the compassionate and generous nation I know we truly are. And it's shocking that Christians, who are held to a higher standard by our Lord, are praying even less for refugees." "We believe that our nation can continue to be both compassionate and secure," a group of evangelical leaders said in a public letter. They emphasized the call to love your neighbor as yourself and to do unto others as you would have them do to you.

Other evangelical leaders, such as Franklin Graham, pushed back. They insisted that refugees needed to be vetted "to be sure their philosophies related to freedom and liberty are in line with ours." In general, evangelical leaders are more likely to oppose bans on Muslims, while lay evangelicals are more likely to support bans.

The evidence indicates that a complex mix of factors shapes American views of Muslim immigrants and refugees. Attitudes among different religious, political, and racial-ethnic groups vary significantly. The same true regarding Irish-Catholic immigrants 175 years ago. Visions of an America that is Christian and white remain powerful. Even American Catholics, once members of a religion deemed incompatible with American values, have expressed support of bans on Muslim immigrants and refugees.

"Strangers
in the Land"

8

The history of immigration debates echoes in the present. History is not just an exercise in curiosity or nostalgia because the past is still with us. Learning history can help us to better understand where we are today. The history of debates about immigration can help us to reflect on how we should approach "strangers in the land" (see Exodus 23:9 KJV) in our own time.

We can learn something about ourselves when we examine our ancestors and their values. Unless you are Native American or an immigrant, your ancestors include both native-born and immigrant Americans, depending how far back you go. We also can think about what our values call us to do today. Religious texts like the Bible and ideals of natural rights and human rights remind us that we are more than citizens of a particular nation.

What can we learn from the past about our debates today about immigrants and refugees? How can we bring normative values, whether American political ideals or the biblical call to love God and neighbor, to both this history and debates today?

GLOBALIZATION

One insight is that immigration is part of the history of globalization. Barriers to migration broke down in the nineteenth and twentieth centuries. This was true not just for the United States but for other immigrant societies too (e.g., Canada, Argentina, Australia). In the past half century, European countries have also seen significant immigration from Asia and Africa, often from former colonies. The United Nations and international law structured the new global relations and promoted international values. Businesses went global, with investment, labor, and goods flowing across national borders. The Christian church became global too. Missionaries grew skeptical of bringing their "civilization" as well as the gospel to new peoples. Instead, they began to help local people around the world make Christianity their own, on their own terms. Immigrants and refugees to the United States today often bring their own forms of Christianity with them.

It would be easy to make this story sound like progress and redemption. But nativism and racism have not disappeared. It also is not clear whether immigration policies designed in the nineteenth and twentieth centuries are adequate for dealing with problems of the twenty-first.

An important example is climate change. Rising sea levels and drought caused by climate change could create tens of millions of displaced persons, perhaps hundreds of millions. That is many more than the 71 million in 2020. Some of those displaced people will be able to move within their nations, but many will be forced to migrate to nearby countries and around the world. Managing both desperate refugees and other immigrants will be a challenging moral and practical issue for countries around the world. The challenge may lead to political and military crises in some regions. How will governments and international organizations manage the flow of people across borders and help receiving countries absorb displaced people? Countries will need to cooperate to maintain economic, social, and political stability. They will not be able to do this on their own, even wealthy, powerful ones like the United States.

In the long run, kingdoms, nations, and empires have never been able to resist migration. Borders have always been porous. They are as much frontiers where people meet as barriers that keep them apart. The biblical story of Jacob and his family fleeing famine and seeking food in Egypt is a familiar example. Jacob's descendants caused fear among Egypt's rulers a few generations later. The end of the Bronze Age in the Mediterranean region was a time of invasions and migrations by various peoples into Egypt and Canaan, the Israelites among them.

In the promised land, the prophets repeatedly told the Israelites to welcome the stranger, as they had been strangers in Egypt. The repetition of the command in the Scriptures suggests that the Israelites often failed to welcome strangers and needed to be reminded.

RACE AND POWER

A second insight is that anti-immigrant sentiment is connected to other issues of race and power. In the nineteenth and early twentieth centuries, white dominance meant controlling immigration, segregating African Americans, forcing Native Americans onto reservations, and pushing aside Mexican Americans. White dominance also required preventing workers from different ethnic, racial, and religious groups from uniting in labor unions against their employers.

Opponents of immigration today generally do not use overt racial language. They often agree that racism is wrong. Only extremists use the kind of crude racist language that was common in the late 1800s and early 1900s. But we can hear coded echoes of racial language from the past. Anti-immigrant activists today talk about "demographic changes" and saving Western civilization. "In some parts of the country it does seem like the America we know and love doesn't exist anymore," said TV and radio talk show host Laura Ingraham on *Fox News*. "Massive demographic changes have been foisted upon the American people. And they're changes that none of us ever voted for and most of us don't like."

This coded language echoes the nativism of the past. Who is the "we" that Ingraham speaks for? People of color and people who are not Christian, whether immigrant or native-born, recognize that this "we" does not include them. They are the "demographic changes" that Ingraham opposes, in an America that will be majority persons of color sometime in the next forty years or so, leaving whites a minority.

CONFLICT AND ADAPTATION

A third insight involves patterns of conflict and adaptation. The United States is a nation of immigrants. But immigrants from one generation often feared new immigrants a generation or two later. In the 1830s to 1850s, nativists viewed the Irish as a racial threat. Irish Americans soon viewed Chinese immigrants and then Jewish immigrants as racial threats. And so on. Racial and ethnic status was relative. Once people achieved a higher status—that is, were accepted as "white"—they often defended it loudly.

The same was true of religion. Nativists like Samuel Morse insisted that Roman Catholics hated freedom and could not be loyal Americans. Today five of our nine Supreme Court justices are Catholic. Catholics embrace democracy like other Americans do. They come from diverse ethnic and racial backgrounds, often mixed through intermarriage. They disagree with one another about issues—including immigration—as much as they disagree with people from other religious backgrounds. The same is true of Mormons. Once a despised religious minority, they are now mainstream Americans just like Catholics.

The repeated pattern is not just about conflict. It is also about adaptation. Native-born Americans and new immigrant groups repeatedly have adjusted to one another. This is a shared American story. It includes conflict, even violence, but it has been one of adaptation in the long run.

Native-born Protestants and immigrant Jews and Roman Catholics became more familiar with one another.

After World War II, Protestants made room for "Christian" America to include Catholics. Christians and Jews began to talk about the United States as having a "Judeo-Christian" heritage. Immigrant religious groups, meanwhile, figured out how to be faithful to their traditions and embrace American ideals of religious liberty.

A non-immigrant parallel is the history of Mormons in the United States. That history includes vigilante violence on both sides. It includes the government jailing Mormon leaders for refusing to end plural marriage (polygamy). It includes Mormons changing their views of plural marriage. And it includes non-Mormons accepting Mormons as part of American life. Both religious traditions and American politics have evolved.

Accommodation has always involved struggle. But the vision of who can be an American has widened over time. Ideas like America as a melting pot and multiculturalism indicate this. Conflicts over immigration were traumatic. Despite them, and sometimes because of them, native-born and immigrant Americans generally learned to live with one another. But as current debates indicate, we continue to struggle with what it means to be American and what this means for immigrants and immigration policy.

ECHOES OF THE PAST IN THE PRESENT

With this history in mind, we should listen for echoes in debates today about being Muslim and American, whether native-born or immigrant. The fears expressed about Muslims today are almost word for word those directed at Roman Catholics in generations past. Like Catholics 175 years ago, Muslims today welcome the freedom to practice their religion. But as Catholics did in the 1800s, they wonder what to do with this freedom when it doesn't seem to fit Muslim thought and habits. And like other Americans, they worry about whether freedom might lead to moral and social disorder. Their desire for liberty and their concern about its consequences are very American. After all, Protestant fears about Catholic immigrants reflected the same worries.

Joseph Keppler, "Looking Backward," cartoon in *Puck*, January 11, 1893. The caption, "They would close to the newcomer the bridge that carried them and their grandfathers over," reveals the irony of old immigrants opposing "new immigrants" from southern and eastern Europe. *The Ohio State University, Billy Ireland Cartoon Library and Museum.*

History cannot tell us how recent Muslim immigrants will adapt to the United States or how native-born Americans will adapt to Muslims. But we can learn from the recurring fear of religious minorities. We can check our fears and remind ourselves that religious minorities have adapted to American life. And we can reflect on the irony that historic religious minorities themselves often feared new minorities.

When we cringe at what Protestants said about Catholics 175 years ago, we should look in the mirror and ask whether we should cringe at what is said about Muslims today, whether we should cringe at what we say or our families or neighbors say. We have heard these things before. And we should ask, How we can best help, or simply make room for, today's immigrants to adapt to American life? After all, they don't hate or fear freedom any more than we do.

Much the same is true about ethnicity and race. What echoes of animosity toward Irish or Italian immigrants in the past can we hear in what is directed at Mexican and Central American immigrants today?

MORAL FRAMEWORKS

In 1960, Father John Courtney Murray discussed Christian perspectives on democracy and pluralism in *We Hold These Truths: Catholic Reflections on the American Proposition*. For "the citizen who is also a Christian," Murray observed, "there resides the consciousness" that "every foreign land is a fatherland and every fatherland is a foreign land." Murray was quoting an early Christian document, *Letter to Diognetes*, from the second century after Christ.

Murray's insight was that, as Christians, we should be both at home and strangers in any city, nation, or empire. We can be Greek or Roman or American. But we also have another allegiance, a greater one, to a higher power than any nation or state. Both allegiances call us to see and to live beyond our narrow horizons. All people are created equal, not just those of one sex, race, nation, or religion. We are to be hospitable to the stranger, as we have been strangers. And, in loving God before all else, we are to love our neighbors as ourselves.

Such values do not lead in obvious ways to specific, practical policies. But they do set moral boundaries for immigration policies.

Notes

Series Editor's Foreword

7   *Midway along the journey of our life:* The opening verse of
Dante Alighieri, *The Inferno*, trans. Mark Musa (Bloomington:
Indiana University Press, 1995), 19.

8   **"We are always on the road":** From Calvin's thirty-fourth ser-
mon on Deuteronomy (5:12–14), preached on June 20, 1555
(*Ioannis Calvini Opera quae supersunt Omnia*, ed. Johann-
Wilhelm Baum et al. [Brunsvigae: C. A. Schwetschke et Filium,
1883], 26.291), as quoted in Herman Selderhuis, *John Calvin:
A Pilgrim's Life* (Downers Grove, IL: InterVarsity, 2009), 34.

8   **"a gift of divine kindness":** From the last chapter of John
Calvin, *Institutes of the Christian Religion, 1541 French Edition*,
trans. Elsie Anne McKee (Grand Rapids: Eerdmans, 2009),
704. Titled "Of the Christian Life," the entire chapter is a guide
to wise and faithful living in this world.

Chapter 1

15 **"Our institutions," he claimed:** Samuel Morse, *Foreign Conspiracy Against the Liberties of the United States* (New York:
Leavitt, Lord, 1835), 59.

16 **"suspect them all":** Samuel Morse, *Imminent Dangers to
the Free Institutions of the United States through Foreign*

Immigration, and the Present State of the Naturalization Laws
(New York: E.B. Clayton, 1935), 24.

17 "Now I have God's body in my pocket": Stephen Waldman,
*Sacred Liberty: America's Long, Bloody, and Ongoing Struggle
for Religious Freedom* (New York: HarperOne, 2019), 66.

19 "The vital principle of democracy" John Ireland, "Abraham
Lincoln: The Savior of the Union—The Exemplar of Democ-
racy," in Ireland, *The Church and Modern Society*, vol. 2 (St.
Paul: Pioneer Press, 1905), 140. Speech given in Chicago in
February 1903. Quoted in Timothy Brunk, "American Excep-
tionalism in the Thought of John Ireland," *American Catholic
Studies* 119, no. 1 (Spring 2008): 48.

Chapter 2

25 family of John Kearney: Kerby A. Miller, *Emigrants and
Exiles: Ireland and the Irish Exodus to North America* (New
York: Oxford University Press, 1985), 496.

26 Some 4.8 million people emigrated from Britain and Europe:
United States Department of Homeland Security, *Yearbook of
Immigration Statistics: 2008* (Washington, D.C.: U.S. Department
of Homeland Security, Office of Immigration Statistics, 2009), 6,
https://www.dhs.gov/sites/default/files/publications/Yearbook
_Immigration_Statistics_2008.pdf (accessed May 15, 2020).

26 "Popery is a *Political system*": Samuel Morse, *Foreign Conspiracy Against the Liberties of the United States* (New York:
Leavitt, Lord, 1835), 118.

28 The percentage of foreign-born people in the United States:
This information comes from the United States Census. A
table for the immigrant population can be found in "History
of Immigration to the United States," Wikipedia, https://en
.wikipedia.org/wiki/History_of_immigration_to_the_United
_States (accessed March 2, 2020).

29 the population of Ireland: These numbers are widely cited. A table of the numbers can be found in "Irish Population Analysis," Wikipedia, https://en.wikipedia.org/wiki/Irish_population _analysis (accessed March 2, 2020).

30 The northeastern states were the most urban: This information comes from the United States Census. A table for rural-urban populations can be found in "Urbanization in the United States," Wikipedia, https://en.wikipedia.org/wiki /Urbanization_in_the_United_States#Historical_statistics (accessed March 2, 2020).

34 As many as 5 million Americans: Historians' estimates range from 1.5 to 5 million. The Klan itself reported 5 million by 1926. See Nancy MacLean, *Behind the Mask of Chivalry: The Making of the Second Klan* (New York: Oxford University Press, 1994), 10, 197.

35 "I believe in an America": Stephen Waldman, *Sacred Liberty: America's Long, Bloody, and Ongoing Struggle for Religious Freedom* (New York: HarperOne, 2019), 229.

Chapter 3

39 "I hope you will pardon": John R. Wunder, *Gold Mountain Turned to Dust: Essays on the Legal History of the Chinese in the Nineteenth-Century American West* (Albuquerque: University of New Mexico Press, 2018), 17.

43 A mob of white miners: Clayton D. Laurie, "Civil Disorder and the Military in Rock Springs, Wyoming: The Army's Role in the 1885 Chinese Massacre," *Montana: The Magazine of Western History* 40, no. 3 (September 1990): 44–59.

43 "If the ballot fails": Jean Pfaelzer, *Driven Out: The Forgotten War Against Chinese Americans* (Berkeley: University of California Press, 2008), 78.

50 "It is repentance": Wunder, *Gold Mountain Turned to Dust*, 72.

50 **"an actual clear and present danger":** Wunder, *Gold Mountain Turned to Dust*, 75–76.

Chapter 4

53 **"Will we extend the hand of Christian brotherhood":** Howard Grose, *Aliens or Americans?* (New York: Young People's Missionary Movement, 1906), 10–11.

54 **"The immigrant comes into a new environment":** Grose, *Aliens or Americans?*, 297.

54 **"Unguarded Gates":** Grose, *Aliens or Americans?*, 3.

57 **In the 1850s, 2.8 million immigrants arrived:** *Yearbook of Immigration Statistics: 2008*, 6-8.

59 **Advocates of "eugenics":** Daniel Okrent, *The Guarded Gate: Bigotry, Eugenics and the Law That Kept Two Generations of Jews, Italians, and Other European Immigrants Out of America* (New York: Scribner, 2019).

64 **In "Trans-National America," in the *Atlantic Monthly*:** Randolph S. Bourne, "Trans-National America," *The Atlantic Monthly*, July 1916, 97.

Chapter 5

70 **In 1940, 1941, and 1942, polls found:** Theodore S. Hamerow, *Why We Watched: Europe, America, and the Holocaust* (New York: Norton, 2008), 202.

70 **"did the right thing when he took away the power of the Jews":** Hazel Gaudet Erskine, "The Polls: Religious Prejudice, Part 2: Anti-Semitism," *Public Opinion Quarterly* 29, no. 4 (Winter 1965–66): 663.

71 **over 165 million displaced persons:** For the numbers in the following paragraphs, see Peter Gatrell, *The Making of the Modern Refugee* (New York: Oxford University Press, 2013), 2-3.

74 **"well-founded fear of being persecuted":** Article 1 of UN General Assembly, *Convention Relating to the Status of Refugees,* July 28, 1951, United Nations, Treaty Series, vol. 189, https://www.refworld.org/docid/3be01b964.html (accessed March 7, 2020).

75 **More than 18 million people:** "U.S. Immigration Since 1965," History, June 7, 2019, https://www.history.com/topics /immigration/us-immigration-since-1965 (accessed May 15, 2020). For immigration numbers in this era generally, see *Yearbook of Immigration Statistics: 2008,* 6-8.

76 **"In 1965, 84%":** "Modern Immigration Wave Brings 59 Million to U.S., Driving Population Growth and Change Through 2065: Views of Immigration's Impact on U.S. Society Mixed," Pew Research Center, September 28, 2015, 9, https://www. pewresearch.org/hispanic/wp-content/uploads/sites/5/2015 /09/2015-09-28_modern-immigration-wave_REPORT.pdf (accessed March 7, 2020).

Chapter 6

81 **In 1953, activists from the American GI Forum:** Erin Blakemore, "The Largest Mass Deportation in American History," *History,* June 18, 2019, https://www.history.com/news/operation -wetback-eisenhower-1954-deportation (accessed March 15, 2020).

91 In 1990, it remained about 2 million: Jeffrey S. Passel and D'Vera Cohn, "Mexicans Decline to Less than Half the U.S. Unauthorized Immigrant Population for the First Time," Pew Research Center, June 12, 2019, https://www.pewresearch.org /fact-tank/2019/06/12/us-unauthorized-immigrant-population -2017/ (accessed May 16, 2020).

93 **From a peak of 12.2 million unauthorized immigrants in 2007:** Jens Manuel Krogstad, Jeffrey S. Passel, and D'Vera Cohn, "5 facts about illegal immigration in the U.S.," Pew

Research Center, June 12, 2019, https://www.pewresearch.org
/fact-tank/2019/06/12/5-facts-about-illegal-immigration-in-the
-u-s/ (accessed May 16, 2020).

94 The number of deportees reached a high: Alex Nowrasteh,
"Deportation Rates in Historical Perspective," *Cato Institute*,
September 16, 2019, https://www.cato.org/blog/deportation
-rates-historical-perspective (accessed March 15, 2020).

94 The shift under President Donald Trump: The Editorial
Board, "All Presidents Are Deporters in Chief," *New York Times*,
July 13, 2019, https://www.nytimes.com/2019/07/13/opinion
/sunday/trump-deportations-immigration.html (accessed
March 15, 2020).

94 including targeting families: Nick Miroff, "ICE raids targeting migrant families slated to start Sunday in major U.S.
cities," *The Washington Post*, June 21, 2019, https://www.
washingtonpost.com/immigration/ice-raids-targeting-migrant
-families-slated-to-start-sunday-in-major-us-cities/2019/06/21
/f2936318-942e-11e9-b570-6416efdc0803_story.html
(accessed May 15, 2020).

95 A Pew Research poll in 2018: Madeline Fry, "An Old Poll
Indicates Evangelicals Don't Care about Refugees. How
Do They Actually Feel?," *Washington Examiner*, July 9,
2019, https://www.washingtonexaminer.com/opinion/
an-old-poll-indicates-evangelicals-dont-care-about-refugees-
how-do-they-actually-feel (accessed March 15, 2020).

95 A similar divide exists: Ulrike Elisabeth Stockhousen, "Evangelicals and Immigration: A Conflicted History," *Process: A
Blog for American History*, March 18, 2019, http://www.
processhistory.org/stockhausen-immigration/ (accessed
March 15, 2020).

95 Hispanic evangelicals are more likely: Ryan Burge, "Are Hispanics Changing the Face of Evangelical Politics?," *Religion in*

Public, March 27, 2018, https://religioninpublic.blog/2018/03
/27/are-hispanics-changing-the-face-of-evangelical-politics/
(accessed March 15, 2020).

95 **Y. Liz Dong and Ben Lowe:** Fry, "An Old Poll Indicates
Evangelicals Don't Care about Refugees. How Do They Actually
Feel?"

95 **Reverend Robert Jeffress:** "Read the Sermon Donald Trump
Heard Before Becoming President," *Time*, January 20, 2017,
https://time.com/4641208/donald-trump-robert-jeffress
-st-john-episcopal-inauguration/ (accessed March 15, 2020).

96 **Demographic trends indicate:** Jens Manuel Kroogstad, "A
View of the Nation's Future through Kindergarten Demo-
graphics," Pew Research Center, July 31, 2019, https://www.
pewresearch.org/fact-tank/2019/07/31/kindergarten
-demographics-in-us/ (accessed March 15, 2020). For projections with different immigration scenarios, see Sandra
Johnson, "A Changing Nation: Population Projections Under
Alternative Immigration Scenarios," United States Census
Bureau, February 2020, https://www.census.gov/content/dam
/Census/library/publications/2020/demo/p25-1146.pdf
(accessed March 15, 2020).

Chapter 7

99 **People refer to one Paterson neighborhood:** Zahra Hankir,
"Immigrants Are Reviving Paterson, N.J., from Its Difficult
Past," *Los Angeles Times*, September 26, 2019, https://www.
latimes.com/world-nation/story/2019-09-25/immigrants-are-
reviving-south-paterson-n-j-from-its-difficult-past (accessed
March 15, 2020).

99 **These claims have been debunked:** Lauren Carroll, "Fact-
Checking Trump's Claim That Thousands in New Jersey
Cheered When World Trade Center Tumbled," *Politifact*,
November 22, 2015, https://www.politifact.com/factchecks

/2015/nov/22/donald-trump/fact-checking-trumps-claim
-thousands-new-jersey-ch/ (accessed March 15, 2020).

100 **About 15 percent of slaves:** "Islam Has Been a Piece of the
American Religious Fabric Since the First Settlers Arrived in
North America," *Smithsonian*, https://nmaahc.si.edu/explore
/stories/collection/african-muslims-early-america (accessed
March 15, 2020).

100 **An example is Omar ibn Said:** Michael E. Ruane, "When
Few Enslaved People in the United States Could Write, One
Man Wrote His Memoir in Arabic," *Washington Post*, January
20, 2019, https://www.washingtonpost.com/history/2019
/01/20/when-few-enslaved-people-could-write-one-man
-wrote-his-memoirs-arabic/ (accessed March 15, 2020).

101 **"the religious rights of the 'Mahamdan'":** Jennifer Williams,
"A Brief History of Islam in America," *Vox*, January 29, 2017,
https://www.vox.com/2015/12/22/10645956/islam-in
-america (accessed March 15, 2020).

101 **90 percent of which was Christian:** Alixa Naff, *Becoming
American: The Early Arab Immigrant Experience* (Carbon-
dale: Southern Illinois University Press, 1993), 2.

101 **African Americans make up one-fifth of Muslims:** Besheer
Mohamed and Jeff Diamant, "Black Muslims Account for a
Fifth of All U.S. Muslims, and about Half Are Converts to
Islam," Pew Research Center, January 17, 2019, https://www.
pewresearch.org/fact-tank/2019/01/17/black-muslims-account
-for-a-fifth-of-all-u-s-muslims-and-about-half-are-converts-to
-islam/ (accessed March 15, 2020).

102 **Immigrants from these parts of the world:** Moni Basu,
"15 Years after 9/11, Sikhs Still Victims of Anti-Muslim Hate
Crimes," *CNN*, September 15, 2016, https://www.cnn.com
/2016/09/15/us/sikh-hate-crime-victims/index.html
(accessed March 15, 2020).

102 **Today Muslims make up 1 percent:** Jeffrey S. Passel and D'Vera Cohn, "U.S. Population Projections: 2005–2050," Pew Research Center, February 11, 2008, https://www.pewsocial trends.org/2008/02/11/us-population-projections-2005-2050/ (accessed March 15, 2020).

103 **According to a 2018 Pew Research survey:** Hannah Hartig, "Republicans Turn More Negative toward Refugees as Number Admitted to U.S. Plummets," Pew Research Center, May 24, 2018, https://www.pewresearch.org/fact-tank/2018/05/24 /republicans-turn-more-negative-toward-refugees-as-number -admitted-to-u-s-plummets/ (accessed March 15, 2020).

105 **"We should invade their countries":** Ann Coulter, "This Is War," *Townhall*, September 14, 2001, https://townhall.com /columnists/anncoulter/2001/09/14/this-is-war-n865496 (accessed March 7, 2020).

106 **"Our motto should be after 9/11":** Ann Coulter, "Muslim Bites Dog," *Townhall*, February 15, 2006, https://townhall. com/columnists/anncoulter/2006/02/15/muslim-bites-dog -n954323 (accessed March 7, 2020).

106 **Since 2017, President Donald Trump:** George Hawley, "Ambivalent Nativism: Trump Supporters' Attitudes toward Islam and Muslim Immigration," *Brookings*, July 24, 2019, https://www.brookings.edu/research/ambivalent-nativism -trump-supporters-attitudes-toward-islam-and-muslim -immigration/ (accessed March 15, 2020).

106 **As a candidate and president:** Tyler Anbinder, "Trump Has Spread More Hatred of Immigrants than Any American in History," *Washington Post*, November 7, 2019, https://www. washingtonpost.com/outlook/trump-has-spread-more-hatred -of-immigrants-than-any-american-in-history/2019/11/07/7 e253236-ff54-11e9-8bab-0fc209e065a8_story.html (accessed March 15, 2020).

106 **This rhetoric includes attacks:** Martin Pengelly, "'Go Back Home': Trump Aims Racist Attack at Ocasio-Cortez and Other Congresswomen," *Guardian*, July 15, 2019, https://www. theguardian.com/us-news/2019/jul/14/trump-squad-tlaib -omar-pressley-ocasio-cortez (accessed March 15, 2020.)

107 **According to a poll in 2019:** Dalia Mogahed and Azka Mahmood, "American Muslim Poll 2019: Predicting and Preventing Islamophobia," Institute for Social Policy and Understanding, 2019, 19–20, https://www.ispu.org /american-muslim-poll-2019-full-report/ (accessed March 15, 2020).

107 **A poll in 2015 found that 76 percent of Republicans:** Robert P. Jones, Daniel Cox, Betsy Cooper, and Rachel Lienesch, *Anxiety, Nostalgia, and Mistrust: Findings from the 2015 American Values Survey* (Washington, DC: Public Religion Research Institute, 2015), 28, https://www.prri.org /wp-content/uploads/2015/11/PRRI-AVS-2015.pdf (accessed March 18, 2020).

108 **Native-born Muslim Americans:** "Muslims in America: Immigrants and Those Born in U.S. See Life Differently in Many Ways," Pew Research Center, April 17, 2018, https:// www.pewforum.org/essay/muslims-in-america-immigrants -and-those-born-in-u-s-see-life-differently-in-many-ways/ (accessed March 15, 2020).

109 **"It's disappointing to see America's heart":** Lois Beckett, "Evangelical Christian leaders: travel ban violates religious beliefs on refugees," *Guardian*, January 30, 2017, https:// www.theguardian.com/us-news/2017/jan/30/evangelical -christians-trump-travel-ban-christian-refugees (accessed March 15, 2020).

109 **"We believe that our nation":** Elana Schor and Seung Min Kim, "Christian Groups Oppose Trump's Preference for

Christian Refugees," *Politico*, January 29, 2017, https://www.politico.com/story/2017/01/trump-immigration-christians-234341 (accessed March 15, 2020).

109 **"to be sure their philosophies":** Laurie Goodstein, "Christian Leaders Denounce Trump's Plan to Favor Christian Refugees," *New York Times*, January 29, 2017, https://www.nytimes.com/2017/01/29/us/christian-leaders-denounce-trumps-plan-to-favor-christian-immigrants.html (accessed March 15, 2020).

109 **lay evangelicals are more likely:** Tara Isabella Burton, "The Bible Says to Welcome Immigrants. So Why Don't White Evangelicals?" *Vox*, October 30, 2018, https://www.vox.com/2018/10/30/18035336/white-evangelicals-immigration-nationalism-christianity-refugee-honduras-migrant (accessed March 15, 2020).

110 **Even American Catholics:** Rhina Guidos, "Survey Shows Views on Immigration Differ among Catholics," *Catholic Virginian*, June 24, 2016, https://www.catholicvirginian.org/?p=1931 (accessed March 15, 2020).

Chapter 8

116 **"In some parts of the country"**: Brett Samuels, "Laura Ingraham: America as We Know It Doesn't Exist Anymore Due to 'Demographic Changes,'" *Hill*, August 9, 2018, https://thehill.com/homenews/media/401044-laura-ingraham-america-as-we-know-it-doesnt-exist-anymore-due-to-demographic (accessed March 18, 2020).

120 **"the citizen who is also a Christian"**: John Courtney Murray SJ, *We Hold These Truths: Catholic Reflections on the American Proposition* (1960; repr., Oxford, UK: Rowman & Littlefield, 2005), 31–32.

NOTES FOR ILLUSTRATIONS

Chapter 1

16 "Riot in Philadelphia": H. Bucholzer, "Riot in Philadelphia." Lithograph, June [i.e., July] 7, 1844. Source: Library of Congress Prints and Photographs Division, Washington, DC. 20540 USA. LC-USZ62-3536 (b&w film copy neg.) LC-DIG-pga-05259 (digital file from original item). No known restrictions on publication. https://www.loc.gov/pictures/item/2003654121/ (accessed March 2, 2020).

Chapter 2

29 "The Ignorant Vote": Thomas Nast, "The Ignorant Vote," cartoon in *Harper's Weekly*, December 9, 1876. Source: Library of Congress Prints and Photographs Division Washington, DC. 20540 USA. LC-USZ62-57340 (b&w film copy neg.). No known restrictions on publication. https://www.loc.gov /pictures/item/2005676066/ (accessed March 2, 2020).

Chapter 3

41 "A Picture for Employers": J. Keppler, "A Picture for Employers," cartoon in *Puck*, August 21, 1876. Source: Library of Congress Prints and Photographs Division, Washington, DC. 20540 USA. LC-USZC2-1242 (color film copy slide). https://www.loc .gov/pictures/item/2002720432/ (accessed March 3, 2020).

Chapter 4

56 "Types and Development of Man": "Types and Development of Man," frontispiece to J. W. Buel, ed., *Louisiana and the Fair: An Exposition of the World, Its People, and Their Achievements*, vol. 5 (St. Louis: World's Progress Publishing Company, 1905), i.

61 "The Americanese Wall": Raymond O. Evans, "The Americanese Wall," cartoon in *Puck*, March 25, 1916. Source: Library of Congress Prints and Photographs Division, Washington, DC. 20540 USA. https://www.loc.gov/pictures/item/2006681433/ (accessed March 4, 2020).

Chapter 5

68 "Ashamed!": Fred L. Packer, "Ashamed!," cartoon in *New York Daily Mirror*, June 1939, https://flucht-geschichten.de/nowhere -to-go/wp-content/uploads/sites/2/2018/02/Karikatur-Fred -Packer-976x1024.jpg (accessed March 7, 2020).

Chapter 6

83 "The Republic of Texas and the United States in 1837": *McConnell's Historical Maps of the United States* (Chicago: McConnell Map Co., 1919), map 26. Source: Library of Congress Geography and Map Division, Washington, DC. 20540-4650 USA. https://lccn.loc.gov/2009581130 (accessed March 15, 2020).

83 "Results of the Mexican War": *McConnell's Historical Maps of the United States* (Chicago: McConnell Map Co., 1919), map 30. Source: Library of Congress Geography and Map Division, Washington, DC. 20540-4650 USA. https://lccn.loc.gov /2009581130 (accessed March 15, 2020).

Chapter 7

105 Tweets from President Trump: "In His Own Words: The President's Attacks on the Courts," Brennan Center for Justice, June 5, 2017, https://www.brennancenter.org/our-work /research-reports/his-own-words-presidents-attacks-courts (accessed March 7, 2020).

108 "We the People Are Greater Than Fear": Shepard Fairey, "We the People Are Greater Than Fear," Amplifier, https:// amplifier.org/campaigns/we-the-people/ (accessed March 8, 2020).

Chapter 8

119 "Looking Backward": Joseph Keppler, "Looking Backward,"
cartoon in *Puck*, January 11, 1893. Source: The Ohio State
University, Billy Ireland Cartoon Library and Museum
https://hdl.handle.net/1811/5143aead-56d8-4349-a291-
92639d196bbd (May 14, 2020).

Further Reading

Abdo, Geneive. *Mecca and Main Street: Muslim Life in America after 9/11*. New York: Oxford University Press, 2006.

Bon Tempo, Carl J. *Americans at the Gate: The United States and Refugees during the Cold War*. Princeton: Princeton University Press, 2008.

Daniels, Roger. *Coming to America: A History of Immigration and Ethnicity in American Life*. 2nd ed. New York: Harper Perennial, 2002.

Fea, John. *Was America Founded as a Christian Nation?* Rev. ed. Louisville, KY: Westminster John Knox Press, 2016.

Gabbaccia, Donna. *From the Other Side: Women, Gender, and Immigrant Life in the U.S., 1820–1990*. Bloomington: Indiana University Press, 1995.

GhaneaBassiri, Kambiz. *A History of Islam in America: From the New World to the New World Order*. New York: Cambridge University Press, 2010.

Haddad, Yvonne Yazbeck, Jane I. Smith, and John L. Esposito, eds. *Religion and Immigration: Christian, Jewish, and Muslim Experiences in the United States*. Walnut Creek, CA: AltaMira Press, 2003.

Higham, John. *Strangers in the Land: Patterns of American Nativism, 1860–1925.* Rev. ed. New Brunswick, NJ: Rutgers University Press, 2002.

Hsu, Madeline Y. *The Good Immigrants: How the Yellow Peril Became the Model Minority.* Princeton, NJ: Princeton University Press, 2015

Inazu, John D. *Confident Pluralism: Surviving and Thriving through Deep Difference.* Chicago: University of Chicago Press, 2018.

Lee, Erika. *The Making of Asian America: A History.* New York: Simon & Schuster, 2015.

McGreevy, John T. *Catholicism and American Freedom: A History.* New York: Norton, 2004.

Melkonian-Hoover, Ruth M., and Lyman A. Kellstedt. *Evangelicals and Immigration: Fault Lines Among the Faithful.* Cham, Switzerland: Palgrave Macmillan, 2019.

Miller, Kerby. *Emigrants and Exiles: Ireland and the Irish Exodus to North America.* New York: Oxford University Press, 1988.

Ngai, Mai M. *Impossible Subjects: Illegal Aliens and the Making of Modern America.* Updated ed. Princeton: Princeton University Press, 2014.

Nugent, Walter. *Crossings: The Great Transatlantic Migrations, 1870-1914.* Bloomington: Indiana University Press, 1992.

Sarna, Jonathan. *American Judaism: A History.* 2nd ed. New Haven: Yale University Press, 2019.

Smith, David and Pennylyn Dykstra-Pruim. *Christians and Cultural Difference.* Grand Rapids, MI: Calvin College Press, 2016.

Smith, Rogers M. *Civic Ideals: Conflicting Visions of Citizenship in U.S. History.* New Haven: Yale University Press, 1997.

St. John, Rachel. *Line in the Sand: A History of the Western U.S.-Mexico Border.* Princeton: Princeton University Press, 2011.

Takaki, Ronald. *A Different Mirror: A History of Multicultural America.* Rev. ed. New York: Back Bay Books, 2008.

Vargas, Zaragosa. *Crucible of Struggle: A History of Mexican Americans from Colonial Times to the Present Era.* 2nd ed. New York: Oxford University Press, 2016.

Waldman, Stephen. *Sacred Liberty: America's Long, Bloody, and Ongoing Struggle for Religious Freedom.* New York: HarperOne, 2019.

Whitehead, Andrew L. and Samuel L. Perry. *Taking America Back for God: Christian Nationalism in the United States.* New York: Oxford University Press, 2020.

Zoberg, Aristide R. *A Nation by Design: Immigrant Policy in the Fashioning of America.* Cambridge, MA: Harvard University Press, 2008.